At Issue

Should Governments Negotiate with Terrorists?

Other Books in the At Issue Series:

At Issue

Should Governments Negotiate with Terrorists?

Amanda Hiber, Book Editor

GREENHAVEN PRESS
A part of Gale, Cengage Learning

GALE
CENGAGE Learning

Detroit • New York • San Francisco • New Haven, Conn • Waterville, Maine • London

Christine Nasso, *Publisher*
Elizabeth Des Chenes, *Managing Editor*

For more information, contact:
Greenhaven Press
27500 Drake Rd.
Farmington Hills, MI 48331-3535
Or you can visit our Internet site at gale.cengage.com

Articles in Greenhaven Press anthologies are often edited for length to meet page requirements. In addition, original titles of these works are changed to clearly present the main thesis and to explicitly indicate the author's opinion. Every effort is made to ensure that Greenhaven Press accurately reflects the original intent of the authors. Every effort has been made to trace the owners of copyrighted material.

Cover photograph reproduced by permission of Images.com/Corbis.

LIBRARY OF CONGRESS CATALOGING-IN-PUBLICATION DATA

Should governments negotiate with terrorists? / Amanda Hiber, book editor.
    p. cm. -- (At issue)
Includes bibliographical references and index.
ISBN-13: 978-0-7377-3932-9 (hardcover)
ISBN-13: 978-0-7377-3933-6 (pbk.)
1. Terrorism--United States--Prevention--Juvenile literature. 2. Terrorism--Government policy--United States--Juvenile literature. 3. Conflict management--United States-- Juvenile literature. I. Hiber, Amanda.
HV6432.S546 2008
363.325'15610973--dc22
                                                    2008006585

Printed in the United States of America
1 2 3 4 5   12 11 10 09 08

ED141

Contents

Introduction

The questions of whether or not negotiating with terrorists is ethical, or politically effective, have been asked countless times across the globe. This is especially true in the United States since the September 11, 2001, attacks on New York City and Washington, D.C. But as difficult and contentious as these questions are, beneath them is one that is, arguably, even more complex: what makes an organization a *terrorist* organization?

The U.S. Department of State currently lists forty-two organizations as Foreign Terrorist Organizations (FTOs). Among these is one of the more notorious Islamist groups, Palestinian Hamas. But as surely as the U.S. government designates Hamas a terrorist organization, others question this definition. Juan Cole writes in *Salon*, "From a Palestinian point of view, the fundamentalist Hamas party is a legitimately elected government." Echoing this sentiment in the *Arab-American News*, writer Patrick Seale asks, "Is Hamas, in fact, a terrorist organization or is it a legitimate resistance movement to occupation and oppression?" He goes on, "Hamas certainly carried out suicide attacks against Israeli civilians during the second intifada beginning in 2000, which would qualify it for the terrorist label. But then, during that intifada, Israel killed more than four times as many Palestinians as Hamas and other groups killed Israelis." Why then, Seale seems to ask, is Hamas labeled "terrorist" while Israel is not?

Such questions bring to light the inherent subjectivity of the term "terrorist." Where is the line between a movement to fight oppression and a terrorist group? According to some political analysts, the line lies in the perceived validity of the group's political aims. In his *New York Times* article only weeks after the bombing of London's transport network in July 2005, Alan Cowell writes about "an evolution in the nature of terrorism that has detached acts of violence from the kind of political aims that Western governments find debatable or negotiable." Cowell points to the distinction drawn by former British prime minister Tony Blair:

> In the case of the IRA [Irish Republican Army], Prime Minister Blair said, "the political demands of [Irish] Republicanism are demands that would be shared by many perfectly law-abiding people who are Nationalists in the north, or citizens of the south in Ireland." The demands of Islamic terrorism, he said, are "none that any serious person could ever negotiate on."

Blair implies such a distinction to justify governments' varying reactions to terrorist groups like the IRA (which appears on the State Department's list) and Islamist groups like al Qaeda.

In Florida's *St. Petersburg Times*, Susan Taylor Martin recounts two starkly contrasted simultaneous events in her area: federal agents were closely monitoring University of South Florida professor Sami al-Arian, whom they suspected of supporting Palestinian terrorist groups, in the same month that Sinn Fein [the political wing of the IRA] leader Gerry Adams was the guest of honor at two different Tampa events. Martin writes, "The contrasting attitudes toward Gerry Adams and Al-Arian illustrate the old adage that one man's terrorist is another man's freedom fighter. They also show that the United States doesn't treat all terrorist groups alike—especially when domestic politics come into play." Taylor goes on to suggest that the U.S. government may treat Sinn Fein differently in light of its 1998 peace deal with the Protestant government in Northern Ireland, despite widespread belief that Sinn Fein is the political counterpart of the IRA. She also questions whether the power of the Israel lobby in the United States plays a part in the government's response to Islamist groups.

There are undoubtedly dozens of factors at play in designating an organization terrorist or otherwise. No matter how this question is answered, the answer is key to a government's decision to negotiate with the organization in question or not. It is not, however, the only question. Governments also closely examine the group's stated demands, past negotiating record, and other elements of the political context when making such a decision. These and many other issues are discussed in *At Issue: Should Governments Negotiate with Terrorists?* These issues are crucial to civilization as more and more citizens live in fear of terrorist attacks, and their governments search for the most effective methods to prevent such attacks.

Governments Should Negotiate with Alleged Terrorists in Some Situations

Noah Feldman

Noah Feldman is a professor of law at Harvard University Law School and a frequent contributor to the New York Times. *He has authored several books, including* After Jihad: America and the Struggle for Islamic Democracy *and* What We Owe Iraq: War and the Ethics of Nation Building.

While many of the United States's allies, such as Great Britain, and pronounced enemies, such as Iran, are conducting negotiations, the United States stands on the sidelines. The U.S. government's policy of not talking with governments and organizations that it deems to be terrorists seems futile, at best. At worst, it wastes an opportunity to create real change in these regimes and can even be dangerous, as in the case of North Korea, which built up an impressive nuclear arsenal while the United States refused to negotiate with its leaders. Ultimately, there is more to be gained through talking than through force, which has been demonstrated in both the 9/11 attacks and the ongoing Israeli-Palestinian conflict. The U.S. government's refusal to talk with Hamas and Iran and others has had real costs, and the government should seriously consider revising its policy on negotiations to prevent further exacerbating these conflicts.

After a summer of protracted and mostly pointless bombing, the talking season is upon us. Unable or unwilling to halt Qassam rocket attacks on Israel and starved for funds, Hamas [Palestinian Sunni Muslim organization elected in 2006 as the government of the Palestinian people] has begun discussing a national unity government with its rival Mahmoud Abbas [president of the Palestinian National Authority and member of the Fatah Party]. Tony Blair [prime minister of Great Britain from 1997 until June 27, 2007,] is rather bravely using his last months in office trying to get Abbas to sit down with the Israelis, who themselves have little to show for their campaign against Hezbollah [Shi'a Islamic political organization based in Lebanon]. Iran, which spent the [2006] summer ignoring barely veiled bombing threats, seems poised to discuss its nuclear program with a coalition that includes China, Russia, Britain, France and Germany.

Conspicuously absent from any of these negotiations is the United States. We approve of all of them, and our diplomats are doubtless in the loop. But officially speaking, silence is our policy. We do not speak with Hamas because of its terrorist activities and unwillingness to recognize Israel's right to exist. In the case of Iran, the trouble stretches all the way back to the 1979–81 hostage crisis, during which we refused to recognize the Islamic Republic. In the latest cycle of tensions over Iran's nuclear progress, the U.S. refuses to join any talks unless Iran first suspends uranium enrichment—which was also the position of our partners until they announced they would be willing to start talking anyway. President [George W.] Bush put his position bluntly last month [September 2006]: "I have made it clear to the Iranian regime that we will sit down with the Iranians once they verifiably suspend their enrichment program. I meant what I said."

What's the point of not talking, especially when others are talking for us? If politics is the art of compromise, then surely conversation is one of its methods. Of course, some enemies—a Hitler or a Pol Pot—may be so repugnant that the mere prospect of reaching a compromise with them would violate our deepest moral principles. The only time it would be right to hear them out is when they are proposing to surrender. There are radical jihadists who see us in similar terms: they find us repellent and see little point in speaking unless it is to warn us of our downfall if we don't submit to their demands. Given their principled unwillingness to compromise, there is little point in talking with them.

Under certain conditions, the motives that drive people and regimes can be changed.

What Can Be Gained

And yet even intractable interlocutors may be worth engaging. Perhaps the conversation serves as a strategy of subterfuge and delay, maintaining a holding pattern or cease-fire until the time is ripe to restart hostilities. Talking can also reveal information about an adversary's leaders—their preconceptions, their blind spots, their fixed beliefs.

Ultimately, however, the most fruitful negotiations are based on a different premise: under certain conditions, the motives that drive people and regimes can be changed. Properly carried out diplomacy creates new incentives that alter countries' underlying interests—and thus their behavior. Over 50 years, a slow and painstakingly negotiated process of economic integration has taught Western Europe's traditional enemies to look upon one another as allies, then friends and now almost as parts of one big country. If there is ever to be a meaningful solution to the Israeli-Palestinian conflict, it will involve something similar: putting both peoples in a position to gain more the closer they come together.

When we put our trust in diplomacy, it is not because it is an inspiring or uplifting discourse or because it helps us see the common humanity in others. The stylized circumlocutions of diplomats can make them seem ridiculous or irrelevant: they never seem to be talking about what is really going on. Moreover, talk between enemies may remind both parties of the depth of their mutual enmities and of all the reasons why they were tempted to use force against one another in the first place.

Nevertheless, diplomacy is essential as long as the use of direct force has limits. After 9/11, most Americans were in no mood to talk with our enemies in the Middle East, whatever those enemies' ideology, and the Bush administration's policies of invasion and pre-emption reflected that sentiment. Now, having relearned the lesson of our limitations, we find ourselves edging back to the table.

Costs of Not Talking

Our refusal to speak with Hamas since its election victory has had real costs. It has suggested to many that our commitment to Middle Eastern democracy is partial at best, and it may have enabled violence by implying that the United States doesn't care all that much about the Israeli-Palestinian conflict. Still, our policy may pay dividends in helping to establish a new Palestinian government, and we should continue to shun Hamas to make sure that such a result occurs. If the new government agrees to abide by previous Palestinian commitments to Israel, however, we should get back to the table quickly.

We need a breakthrough, one that will help either the Israeli-Palestinian track, the Iraq situation or both.

In the case of Iran, the problem is that we are at once desperate for its help in quieting the chaos of Iraq and determined to stop it from developing a nuclear weapon. We have been willing to speak with Iran's leaders about Iraq but not about the weapons—a distinction that Iran regards as arbitrary and has thus far yielded few gains in either realm. We would do better to sit down with Iran now, recalling that by the time we began negotiating with North Korea, its nuclear progress had become all but a fait accompli.

In short, we need a breakthrough, one that will help either the Israeli-Palestinian track, the Iraq situation or both. To get that, we will need the much-maligned diplomats. It could be a British prime minister on his way out, able to accomplish what [former U.S. president] Bill Clinton in his last days could not. It could be the first Muslim secretary general of the United Nations—Prince Zeid al-Hussein of Jordan is a leading candidate—who breaks the impasse. Or it could be the usual suspects, just muddling through and lowering the temperature. In an ideological age, diplomacy may seem weak and prosaic. But sometimes it is all we have.

Governments Should Never Negotiate with Terrorists

Michael Rubin and Suzanne Gershowitz

Michael Rubin is a resident scholar at the American Enterprise Institute (AEI) and editor of Middle East Quarterly. *He is a former political adviser to the Coalition Provisional Authority in Iraq. Suzanne Gershowitz researches foreign policy and defense studies at AEI.*

As the threat of terrorism grows, democratic governments are developing response strategies and, with them, definitions of terrorism. While this should be a simple task, governments complicate it to pacify specific groups or interests. Western governments' beliefs that terrorists will respond to engagement because terrorism is not caused by ideology or religion, is naïve. Terrorists' ideologies often explicitly preclude compromise. Instead of attempting to negotiate with terrorists, governments must marginalize them and render terrorism unprofitable. Disrupting leadership is also a powerful tool. Governments must not be fearful of taking action; terrorists use such fear to their advantage.

Terrorism is a growing threat. The September 11, 2001 attack on the World Trade Center and subsequent attacks on Madrid's Atocha train station and the London underground signaled that 21st century terrorism was not a problem that could be localized to the Middle East and South Asia. As the terror threat grows and groups like Al-Qaeda and

Hezbollah demonstrate worldwide reach, democracies fumble not only for an effective political strategy to combat terrorism, but also for a definition. In order to protect pet interests or excuse specific groups, diplomats and officials complicate what should be a simple definition. Whether in Berlin or Beirut, the definition should be the same: Terrorism is the deliberate targeting of civilians for political gain. Any nuance or justification of the targeting of civilians for political gain merely undercuts efforts to eradicate terrorism.

To combat terrorism effectively, political leaders and diplomats should look not at the terrorists' goals, but rather at their success. After all, terrorism is only a tactic. Adversaries commit terrorist acts when they win more than they lose. Some commit terrorism for publicity, others for ransom, and still others for concession. The key to defeat of terrorism is not through diplomacy, but rather through strategies more forceful and less compromising. Terrorism will cease to be a useful tactic only when its costs become too great for terrorists and their sponsors to bear.

Is Terrorism Ever Legitimate?

Terrorism should never be legitimate. While European politicians, conflict resolution specialists, and some journalists counsel diplomats to address root causes, any group utilizing terror, regardless of their goal, makes their cause illegitimate. The greatest handicap to defeating terrorism today is the assumption that addressing root causes will mitigate the problem. Many seek to twist counter-terror efforts to their own pet cause. Some, for example, say poverty breeds terrorism. This is false. Mali, one of the world's poorest nations is, according to Freedom House, the most democratic Muslim country. It does not produce terrorists.

Nor does lack of opportunity cause terrorism. Most of the September 11, 2001 hijackers were well-educated. Many were engineers. Many suicide bombers likewise have received high school and, in some cases, even university education. Indeed, a twenty-first-century *Modest Proposal* [Seventeenth-century political pamphlet] might interpret data collected about perpetrators of suicide bombings to suggest that stymieing rather than creating educational opportunities could better inhibit recruitment of terrorists.

A third root cause cited by diplomats and scholars is the Israeli-Palestinian conflict. The lack of a final status peace accord, the argument goes, is what causes terror. This too is disingenuous. Terrorism has spiked every time negotiators appear on the brink of Arab-Israeli peace. It was during a declared Palestinian truce, for example, that terrorists sought to import 50 tons of Iranian weaponry, a shipment only stopped when the Israeli navy intercepted the *Karine-A* [freighter carrying the weapons]. Likewise, [al Qaeda terrorist leader] Osama Bin Laden started planning the September 11, 2001 attack on the World Trade Center and the Pentagon just before the Camp David II [Middle East peace] summit [in July 2000], at a time of great optimism in the peace process.

Talk About Causes Is Counterproductive

Discussion of root causes can blur the immorality of terrorism and actually encourage the act. No where was this more evident than when, on April 15, 2002, France, Belgium and four other European Union members endorsed a UN Human Rights Commission resolution condoning "all available means, including armed struggle" to establish a Palestinian state. While publicly declaring their opposition to terrorism, six EU [European Union] members joined the 57-nation Organization of Islamic Conference to legitimize suicide bombing, at least in certain circumstances.

Political adversaries take advantage of the Western obsession with root causes. Terror sponsors extend an olive branch on one hand, but seek to advance their own goals by terrorist proxy on the other. In the midst of Arab-Israeli negotiations in 1993, the Syrian government encouraged Hezbollah to attack Israeli forces in Southern Lebanon. While Iranian president Muhammad Khatami won plaudits in Western capitals for his talk of civilization dialogue, for example, his government continued to fund proxy groups like Islamic Jihad and Hezbollah which worked to advance the Islamic Republic's desire to export revolution and undermine the Middle East peace process.

Legitimizing Terror

Too often Western powers try to make negotiating partners out of dictators and terrorists. Seldom does this curb terrorism. Prior to the September 11, 2001 terrorist attacks, senior State Department official Robin Rafael, for example, counseled the U.S. government to accommodate the Taliban. Diplomatic promises are as ephemeral as terrorists' sincerity. The Taliban embraced engagement to entrench. The Palestinian Authority embraced engagement to rearm. Meanwhile, the Taliban's regime facilitated al-Qaeda and Palestinian Authority leader Yasir Arafat equipped his proxy militias with far more lethal weapons, explosives, and missiles.

The refusal of Arafat to acknowledge agreements made by his negotiators further showed the fallacy of embracing dictators and terror sponsors. The Palestinian Authority made no secret of its willingness to win concession through terror. While Western powers trained the Palestinian police to keep order and prevent terrorism, Palestinian Police Commander Ghazi Jabali told the Palestinian Authority's official newspaper, "The Palestinian police will be leading, together with all other noble sons of the Palestinian people when the hour of confrontation arrives. . . ." On the month anniversary of the collapse of Camp David II, Palestinian Authority Justice Minister Freih Abu Middein, demanding further Israeli concessions, declared, "Violence is near and the Palestinian people are willing to sacrifice even 5,000 casualties."

Turkey's Mistake

Some in the international community risk replicating the mistake with outreach to Hamas. Turkish Prime Minister Recep Tayyip Erdoğan's decision to receive a senior Hamas delegation prior to that group's renunciation of terrorism legitimatized both Hamas and its tactics. Indeed, the Kurdistan Workers Party [PKK], as vicious in its targeting of civilians as Hamas, seized upon the precedent established by Erdoğan. "Is it not blood that is shed in the fighting between the Turkish army and the Kurdistan freedom movement, just like the Palestinian-Israeli conflict?" asked senior PKK commander Murat Karayilan.

Erdoğan's decision has undercut both the Turkish government's own fight against terrorism as well as Ankara's diplomatic leverage should officials in Athens, Nicosia, or other European capitals seek to engage the PKK. He not only legitimized terrorists as negotiating partners, but reaffirmed that the path to political recognition was through the murder of civilians.

The Jihadists [have] learned that violence brings concession.

Negotiation Fallout in Fallujah

The U.S.-led Coalition's willingness to negotiate with terrorists in Iraq has likewise backfired. Between April 6 and April 30, 2004, U.S. Marines surrounded the hotbed town of Fallujah. European officials and human rights groups condemned the U.S. siege. Facing growing international pressure, U.S. forces compromised: They empowered insurgent leaders into a Fallujah Brigade. U.S. Secretary of State Colin Powell explained,

"We want peace in Fallujah, not war in Fallujah. And we won't have to take this to a military climax." Islamists interpreted events differently. Minaret-mounted loudspeakers lauded "victory over the Americans." Rather than bring peace, the decision to compromise sparked an upsurge in violence. The Jihadists learned that violence brings concession. While there were five car bombings during the siege, in the same period following its lifting, there were 30. For the car bombers of Fallujah, the gains of their terror far outweighed its cost.

A Western desire for compromise can also backfire for the simple reason that, while Western officials see their intercession as central to almost every conflict, terrorists do not. At times a group's decision to engage in terror is due as much to local power politics as outside grievance. During the Second Intifada [the second major wave of Palestinian-Israeli violence, beginning in September 2000], groups such as Force-17 and Tanzim took the lead in launching attacks against Israeli targets. The reason was not enhanced grievance relative to other terror groups, but rather a desire for local legitimacy. While the first Intifada raged, Yassir Arafat's Palestine Liberation Organization remained in Tunisian exile. Many West Bank and Gaza Palestinians subsequently resented Arafat's henchmen as illegitimate interlopers imposed on them by outside powers. Arafat used the second Intifada to win local legitimacy through a contest to draw Israeli blood.

A similar dynamic is at work with Hamas now. Hamas rose to popularity in the Gaza Strip and the West Bank as a result of its terror attacks. While some diplomats may also point to its Saudi-subsidized social service network, the fact remains that non-governmental organizations which operated similar programs did not win populist support because of their failure to bomb buses. Hamas terrorism was meant not only to kill Israelis, but also to bolster its own popularity vis-à-vis its rivals. The movement craved publicity, and it received it. It is loathe to lose its populist card.

Rewarding Violence

Further undercutting the fight against terrorism has been Western officials' desire for a peaceful solution regardless of provocation. Even Jerusalem's no-nonsense approach to terrorism has frayed in the face of equivocation and compromise. Any solution short of a violent response to terrorism is akin to rewarding it.

Rewarding violence always backfires. On May 25, 2000, the day after Israel withdrew from southern Lebanon, Shaikh Hassan Nasrallah, the secretary-general of Hezbollah declared, "The road to Palestine and freedom is the road of the resistance and the intifada!" While European and U.S. officials hoped and predicted that withdrawal would curb violence on the south Lebanon-Israeli border, the reality was far different. Hezbollah refused to accept the UN ruling that Israel was in full compliance with UN Security Council Resolution 425 and, instead, simply added new demands.

The willingness of a Western democracy to make concessions . . . has subsequently inspired terrorists in Iraq, Turkey, and India.

More importantly, the precipitous withdrawal demonstrated that Western democracies were weak and would concede to violence. Two months after Israel's pullback, Arafat turned down Israel's offer of a Palestinian state with its capital in Jerusalem, on 97 percent of the West Bank and Gaza and three percent of Israel proper and launched a war designed to strike not only in the West Bank and Gaza, but also in Israel. And so was born the Second Intifada. The impact of the Israeli withdrawal from southern Lebanon went beyond Israel and its neighbors, though. The willingness of a Western democracy to make concessions to improvised explosive devices and mortar attacks has subsequently inspired terrorists in Iraq, Turkey, and India. . . .

Ransom and Hostage-Taking

Hostage-taking has become a particularly effective tactic. Terrorists crave an audience. With the spread of terrorism in the late twentieth century, audiences became inured to violence. Suicide bombings which might once have garnered headlines and commentary for a week now pass with bare mention. For a bombing or slaughter to win significant public attention, it must target children (the Palestine Liberation Organization's slaughter of school children in Ma'alot in 1974 or Chechen Jihadists' seizure of a Beslan school thirty years later); shock (Black September's 1972 massacre of the Israeli Olympic team or the 2006 bombing of the Askariya mosque in Samarra); or result in several thousand casualties, such as occurred on September 11, 2001. Planning and execution of such attacks is difficult and costly. As audiences become increasingly inured to violence, the ability to shock and achieve aims through terror becomes harder. Each incident must surpass the last or it will simply fade into background static. While the Western media once covered every car bombing in Iraq, explosions which claim several dozen lives now seldom get more than a brief mention on television or a couple lines of newspaper print.

Governments have made matters worse by engaging hostage-takers and, in some cases, even paying ransom.

Kidnapping allows terrorists to bypass this dynamic. Hostage-taking extends media attention and allows reporters to humanize the victim. For journalists, an assassination or bombing is anti-climatic; the press only begins its coverage after the operation has ended. But uncertainty about whether a hostage remains alive creates the suspense necessary for a good story. Terrorists have repeatedly used videos of hostages pleading for their lives in order to seize headlines. The plight of freelance journalist Jill Carroll [kidnapped in Iraq in January 2006 and released in March 2006] captivate[d] audiences as each video [was] released and deadline passed.

Talking with Kidnappers Is Dangerous

While negotiating may successfully address the short-term objective of freeing the hostage, without exception, it causes terrorism to proliferate. Dialogue is dangerous. The very act of negotiating, whether directly or through intermediaries, legitimizes the perpetrators and the act. On the twenty-fifth anniversary of the U.S. embassy seizure in Iran, many former hostages reflected upon their ordeal. According to David Roeder, one of the captives, "If we had done something other than just walked away [from Iran at the conclusion of the ordeal], I keep thinking maybe, just maybe, we wouldn't have planted the seed that terrorism is a profitable thing." Terrorism has been very profitable. Kidnapping of Westerners in Lebanon increased in the 1980s after the U.S. and Iran entered into secret talks to win their release.

Governments have made matters worse by engaging hostage-takers and, in some cases, even paying ransom. The Philippines had previous experience with high profile hostage seizure. In March 2000, for example, Libyan leader Muammar al-Qadhafi paid an estimated $25 million ransom to win the release of priests, teachers, and children seized from a school on Basilan Island. While the ransom may have solved a short-term problem, it compounded the long-term terrorist threat. Within months of receiving the ransom, Abu Sayyaf [militant Islamist separatist group based in the Philippines] expanded from a couple hundred to more than a thousand members. The group used the influx of cash to upgrade their equipment. The ransom paid for speedboats and weapons used in subsequent kidnappings.

The pattern is international. In April 2003, Ammari Saifi, the "Bin Laden of the Desert," seized 32 European vacationers in the Algerian desert, holding them captive for 177 days. He released them only after the German government paid a five million euro ransom. Rather than settle for peace, Saifi used the money to buy new vehicles and better weapons. He remains at large and a threat to stability across the Sahel.

A Kidnapping Boom in Iraq

In Iraq, hostage-negotiation has sparked a kidnapping industry. The French and Italian government's decision to ransom its hostages has encouraged further hostage taking. In August 2004, the Iraqi Islamic Army seized two French journalists. Contradicting official denials, a high official in the Direction Générale de la Sécurité Extérieure, France's secret service, confirmed that ransom had been paid. Serge July, editor of left-leaning *Liberation* questioned whether the cost of [French president Jacques] Chirac's political gestures was too high. The Italian government did little better. While the Italian government denied the payment of any ransom for kidnapped Italian journalists Simona Torretta and Simona Pari, Gustavo Selvo, the head of an Italian parliamentary foreign affairs committee, said that there had been a payment of $1 million. He told France's RTL radio, "The lives of the girls was the most important thing. In principle, we shouldn't give in to blackmail, but this time we had to." The terrorists rightly calculated that European leaders were weak. They were right.

Too often, political correctness undercuts the war on terrorism.

How then should Western governments respond to the seizure of hostages? With firmness calculated to defend the long-term safety of both their own citizens and Iraqis. Terrorists do not employ ineffective tactics. The key to defeating the scourge of kidnapping is to make it unprofitable. Sometimes long-term victory trumps short-term tragedy.

The Importance of Ideology

The belief that engagement can moderate terrorists is naïve, for it ignores the importance of ideology. Too often, political correctness undercuts the war on terrorism. It has become fashionable to suggest that religion does not motivate terrorism. The statements of many terrorists—and the last will and testament of the 9-11 hijackers—undercuts such a belief. While foreign policy realists pride themselves on their practicality, they often adhere blindly to the belief that diplomacy and negotiation can resolve any conflict. They may be sincere, but their analysis is undercut by mirror imaging. When Islamist terrorists kidnapped and later beheaded *Wall Street Journal* reporter Daniel Pearl, their goal was to humiliate, not negotiate. Sheer brutality is effective. The video of the beheading of U.S. traveler Nicholas Berg circulated around the world shocking the Iraqis and Westerners alike. There were no demands for his life.

Often terrorists are unwilling to compromise upon ideology. Sheikh Omar Abdel Rahman, mastermind of the first World Trade Center bombing, declared, "There is no truce in Jihad against the enemies of Allah." In other instances, the price of accommodation is too high. In a video tape aired on January 23, 2005, al-Qaeda-in-Iraq leader Abu Musab al-Zarqawi declared, "We have declared a bitter war against democracy." To engage Zarqawi would be counterproductive. No government should be willing to sacrifice democracy for peace. Still, many in the West try, especially when the negotiating chip is not their own society. This too backfires. Engaging ideologues not only legitimizes extremism, but may actually encourage it. If the natural inclination of Western diplomats is to compromise with any demand, why not stake out even more extreme positions?

The Case of Hamas

What does Hamas believe? Article 13 of its Charter makes clear:

[Peace] initiatives, the so-called peaceful solutions, and the international conferences to resolve the Palestinian problem, are all contrary to the beliefs of the Islamic Resistance Movement. For renouncing any part of Palestine means renouncing part of the religion; the nationalism of the Islamic Resistance Movement is part of its faith, the movement educates its members to adhere to its principles and to raise the banner of Allah over their homeland as they fight their Jihad.

It should simply never be acceptable to open negotiations with any group whose goal is the destruction of a state or a people.

It should simply never be acceptable to open negotiations with any group whose goal is the destruction of a state or a people. Unfortunately, the willingness to engage Hamas politically or—in the case of Jacques Chirac's government—financially has undercut the moral clarity of the fight against terrorism and encouraged more. Unfortunately, here Hamas is more the rule rather than the exception. European governments and self-described peace activists still continue to engage Hezbollah, even after the group's leader, Sheikh Hassan Nasrallah, declared, "If they [the Jews] gather in Israel, it will save us the trouble of going after them worldwide." It does not make sense to excuse an organization that stands by such principles in the midst of a battle against terror and a fight for peace.

Effective Counterterrorism

How then can governments counter terrorism? Ideologues ultimately must be marginalized to the point of impotence, isolated, or eliminated. If Western officials, diplomats, and self-described progressives engage with terrorists, they empower them. Rather than be treated as powerbrokers, Nasrallah and Hamas political bureau chief Khalid Mishaal should be international pariahs. Likewise, engagement with Arafat increased rather than diminished Palestinian terrorism.

Terrorists, whether secular or religious, engage in terrorism for a simple reason: They find it a useful tactic. If the West is to defeat terror, it must raise the cost of terrorism beyond the endurance of terrorists. In this, diplomacy and compromise can be counterproductive. The second Palestinian Intifada was sparked by Israel's willingness to engage in diplomacy and withdrawal from southern Lebanon. It was ended because of Jerusalem's willingness to engage in targeted assassination.

Such forceful measures work on a number of levels. In the short-term, they can disrupt planning for specific attacks. When the Israeli military assassinated Hamas official Umar Sa'adah in July 2001, he was planning a major attack at the Maccabiah Games, the Jewish Olympics. His death foiled the attack.

In the long-term, disrupting leadership weakens terrorist organizations. When terrorist leaders are eliminated, leadership struggles ensue. Rather than spark a cycle of violence, a desire for revenge can exhaust it. After Israel began targeting terrorist leaders, their deputies began rushing revenge attacks. Many of these were ill-prepared and accelerated the exposure and elimination of terror cells. The Israeli government raised the cost of engaging in terrorism beyond what Palestinian supporters could bear. Only with unilateral disengagement did the cost of engaging in terrorism again become worthwhile.

Put Pressure on Terror-Sponsoring States

The same logic works on a state level. Libyan leader Mu'ammar Qadhafi reduced terrorism—at least that directed against the West—after [U.S.] President Ronald Reagan launched an air strike against the North African state in response to a Libyan-sponsored Berlin disco bombing. The Syrian government ceased sheltering PKK leader Abdullah Öcalan after the Turkish military staged exercises along the Syrian border. Likewise, a 1999 Turkish air strike on the Iranian border city of Piranshahr convinced Tehran that using PKK fighters as leverage against the Turkish state might not be in Iran's national interest. President George W. Bush's willingness to oust the Taliban prevented attacks on the U.S. mainland not only by denying al-Qaeda a safe-haven, but also by giving pause to other potential terror sponsors.

Terrorists feed off of diplomatic hand-wringing and fear of a cycle of violence to amplify the cost effectiveness of their attacks.

Still, many governments are afraid to take action. They fear a cycle of violence. Terrorists do not need a reason to attack. The Clinton administration's failure to respond to the 1996 Khobar Towers bombing [in Saudi Arabia] did not prevent the 1998 East Africa embassy bombings, nor did its inaction against al-Qaeda after the 2000 USS *Cole* bombing convince Bin Laden to call off the World Trade Center attack. Indeed, terrorists feed off of diplomatic hand-wringing and fear of a cycle of violence to amplify the cost effectiveness of their attacks.

It may be difficult for democracies to take effective counter terror measures, but it is necessary. Terrorists may exploit public opinion. As Israeli Major General Dan Halouts said, "Israel's democracy is particularly sensitive to the humanitarian aspects of the conflict, and is far more exposed to the media than the regimes of its opponents." The same holds true in the United States, Great Britain, or France. Political leadership should be about protecting national security, not just winning popularity in the weekly opinion poll. Ultimately, investing in short-term force can win long-term security and contain the terrorist scourge. Democratic nations must not forget, though, that they are up against an international community that accommodates terrorists and blames the victims—Western democracies and Israel—for terrorists' actions. If democracies do not defend their own legitimacy, no one will.

3

Negotiations Brought About Peace in Northern Ireland

Michael Ancram

Michael Ancram is a Conservative Party member of the British Parliament. He served in the Northern Ireland office as Parliamentary undersecretary of state and minister of state from 1993 to 1994.

As the conflict in the Middle East continues, the necessity of negotiations becomes clearer. I believe my own experiences as a political minister in Northern Ireland provide valuable insight that can be applied to a Middle East peace process. Despite being told, upon my arrival in 1993, that the conflict in Northern Ireland could never be resolved, I was determined that it could be resolved through dialogue. The Downing Street Declaration of 1993, which merely laid out all parties' grievances and desires, laid the groundwork for negotiations and a ceasefire. We then engaged in exploratory dialogue, whereby talks proceeded without conditions. This approach was successful, as it led to the Good Friday agreement. The outcome of this peace process illustrates that such exploratory dialogue can effectively pave the way for long-term peace.

"It is often a better use of time to talk to your enemies than your friends." So said a wise, experienced and senior Israeli to me a few weeks ago. In a similar vein last summer [2006], following the cessation of hostilities in Lebanon, I wrote in *The Independent*, "It is time to start dancing with wolves, to start talking to terrorists."

Michael Ancram, "Dancing with Wolves: The Importance of Talking to Your Enemies," *Middle East Policy*, vol. 14, Summer 2007, pp. 22–29. Copyright © 2007 Basil Blackwell Ltd. Reproduced by permission of Blackwell Publishers.

We live in an age where there has never been a greater failure by the West to engage in dialogue. The result is an increasing incidence of standoff, fear and violence. Nowhere is this more the case today than in the Middle East.

I am neither a pacifist nor a liberal appeaser. As deputy leader of the British Conservative party I called on my colleagues in Parliament to vote for the invasion of Iraq in 2003, without which vote [British prime minister] Tony Blair would have had no mandate to join the United States in toppling [Iraqi dictator] Saddam Hussein.

I come from what might be described as the Northern Ireland school of conflict resolution. I was sent there as political minister in 1993, after years of troubles and 3,000 dead out of a population of 1.5 million, with many more injured and traumatized. It was as bad and intractable a conflict as any.

While drawing too close an analogy between different conflicts is dangerous, there are lessons in common which can be shared.

I want, therefore, to set out my experiences in Northern Ireland, from which I believe some lessons can be learned, particularly as the process we developed in pursuit of peace had largely to be constructed as I went along.

The Northern Ireland Experience

When I arrived, violence was at a new peak: mass bombings, assassinations, sectarian violence, gun-running and outside interference. No one was talking to anyone, not governments, not parties, not insurgents. I was frequently advised that the problem was intractable, that I was wasting my time, and that the "war" would have to go on until it was won.

We made a different analysis. First, that the war could not be won. Second, that there could be no long-term solution to the problem we were confronting without the eventual involvement of those we were fighting. Third, that even as the fighting continued, we needed to find a means of engaging them. And fourth, that this could only be done by opening dialogue.

The first challenge was how to get in touch. The first step was language; publicly using phrases that we understood from other sources might resonate with the Provisional IRA (Irish Republican Army), which was a proscribed terrorist organisation with whom we were not supposed to talk. The words used were somewhat esoteric, but they were signals. Eventually a signal was received in return: "The war is over, help us to end it." Contact of the barest kind had been made. Meanwhile, the bombings and assassinations continued—if anything, on an intensified scale—and our military response was commensurate.

It was a signal ... aimed at persuading participants that there was sufficient basis for dialogue.

What followed was vicarious dialogue that resulted in a narrative encompassing in general terms the aspirations and grievances of all the participants sufficient to give them a degree of confidence without requiring them to sign on to the others' positions—but equally not to expostulate against them. The outcome was the Downing Street Declaration of December 1993.

There was no prior demand for a cessation of violence or for any undertakings of recognition. It was a signal, ratified by two interested sovereign governments, aimed at persuading participants that there was sufficient basis for dialogue. It was an invitation to engage.

It was designed to encourage the participation of those we needed to bring in, and it set the stage for the ceasefire by the insurgents.

Exploratory Dialogue

Thus the basis for dialogue began to be put in place. A requirement for a permanent renunciation of violence and the decommissioning of illegally held weapons before formal negotiations was bypassed by what became known as exploratory dialogue. More pertinently, there was never a requirement made of Sinn Fein/IRA for de jure recognition of Northern Ireland as part of the United Kingdom. Such a precondition would have been a game-breaker. Exploratory dialogue, talks without conditions or commitment, became the way forward.

In place of negotiating commitments, we were exploring boundaries, establishing lines in the sand beyond which they would not go. Narrow horizons suddenly began to broaden. The hitherto impossible suddenly became remotely possible.

Exploratory dialogue . . . can inch by grinding inch begin to reconcile the apparently irreconcilable.

And there was a vital spin-off. If Sinn Fein/IRA could be persuaded to explore their lines in the sand, why not the democratic parties in the middle and indeed the paramilitaries at the other extreme as well.

It soon became apparent that many of these lines overlapped, albeit without commitment, and that there was scope for progress. This resulted in the informative but nonbinding Framework Document, which demonstrated a way through to a settlement. It was initially disowned by most of the participants but ultimately, because of the robustness of all the gathered lines in the sand, became the basis of the Good Friday agreement.

I have gone to some length in describing the process of exploratory dialogue because I believe the lessons from it are clear and relevant. Dialogue can be achieved even within conflict. Exploratory dialogue can avert the need for preconditions, can inch by grinding inch begin to reconcile the apparently irreconcilable, and seek out the eventual compromises upon which any long-term settlement must inevitably be built.

4

Negotiations Alone Did Not Bring About Peace in Northern Ireland

David Trimble

David Trimble was the first to hold the office of first minister of Northern Ireland (1998–2002). He was awarded the Nobel Peace Prize, with John Hume, in 1998.

Many Europeans believe that terrorism is best dealt with through negotiation, with Northern Ireland often held up as an illustration. Even (former British prime minister) Tony Blair's first Northern Ireland Secretary of State has said that the U.S. and Britain should hold talks with al Qaeda. But to advocate this is to misunderstand the lessons of Northern Ireland. In fact, the Provisional IRA's military defeat in the 1990s paved the way for the subsequent peace process. Even then, some of the advances of the 1998 Good Friday Agreement have disintegrated, in part because the IRA has continued to threaten further violence for its own gain. Future negotiations with the IRA need to make clear that terrorism is no longer acceptable. The terrorist attacks of September 11 reiterated the fact that terrorism must not be tolerated, and that treating terrorists with understanding and compassion is a mistake.

There is an increasingly fashionable assumption in Europe that terrorism cannot be defeated, only appeased through a process of negotiation that concedes core elements of the terrorists' agenda. Northern Ireland is frequently cited as the proof of this assertion. Indeed, Marjorie Mowlam, Tony Blair's first Northern Ireland Secretary of State and now his most disconnected former Cabinet member, has argued that America and Britain should negotiate with al Qaeda. That would be folly and would be to draw entirely the wrong lesson from Northern Ireland. The fact is that the Provisional IRA [Irish Republican Army] suffered a military defeat. [Sinn Fein/IRA president] Gerry Adams might be the most famous Irishman on the planet, but at the price of the collapse of his "long war" strategy.

The objective of the IRA's terrorist campaign since 1970 had been to persuade a British government to coerce the pro-British unionist majority in Northern Ireland, against its will, to enter an independent Irish state. This was a necessary step on the road to its ultimate goal, a Celtic Cuba. By 1994, its leaders knew that aim could not be achieved through terror.

I am not suggesting that the IRA was defeated by firepower alone. On the contrary, after the disaster of "Bloody Sunday" in Londonderry in 1972 [when British soldiers opened fire on Irish protesters], British policy shifted toward an intelligence-led approach and to "Ulsterisation," the concentration of security force operations and responsibility in local hands—if only because of the need for personnel steeped in the local culture. This combined with a refusal to deal politically with the IRA until violence ceased sapped its will to continue the "armed struggle." The IRA managed to sustain very high levels of violence in the 1970s without achieving a breakthrough politically. Their inability to escalate their offensive in the '80s, post-Ulsterisation, set the context for a peace process in the '90s.

Sending a Clear Message

Northern Ireland points up the need for a total strategy, a coordinated approach by all branches of the state. When this strategy broke down, as it did at times in Ulster, it merely delayed the final settlement by giving hope to the terrorists. Key officials, politicians, and even military commanders, occasionally sent apparently emollient signals to the IRA. They gave sustenance to the terrorist campaign. The IRA was encouraged to believe that "one last heave" would see its goals fulfilled.

Above all, the people of Northern Ireland must be allowed to determine their future free from the threat of violence.

All is not rosy in Northern Ireland now. The institutions established under the 1998 Good Friday Agreement have broken down. Yet the principles of that agreement are still sound. Above all, the people of Northern Ireland must be allowed to determine their future free from the threat of violence. An innovative form of power sharing between parties with wildly divergent communal interests was made possible. For almost two years under my leadership as First Minister, Northern Ireland experienced something considered unthinkable only a few years before.

That cross-community government fell, but not through any inherent fault in the structures negotiated in 1998. It fell because the IRA had been allowed to use the threat of a return to violence to extract further concessions. The failure to enforce key terms of the accord encouraged some elements in the IRA to engage in brazen adventures at home and abroad. A return to the armed struggle was impossible, but illegal activity on a significant scale continued both by the IRA and loyalist paramilitaries.

Interestingly, 19th-century British statesmen at times wryly referred to the similarity between dealing with Catholic-Protestant tensions in Ireland and managing Sunni-Shiite relations in Mesopotamia, present-day Iraq. It is vital that both traditions are treated with rigorous fairness. I protested when

British policy leaned towards tolerating one side's illegalities but not the other's. Sunni insurgents and Shiite insurgents must not be treated differentially.

A New World Order

The key question on the eve of another set of negotiations about Northern Ireland is whether Mr. Blair's assessment of the post-9/11 world—that the threat of terrorist violence is no longer acceptable and that the IRA has no option but to disband—is understood and accepted by the IRA leadership. Sept. 11 transformed the terms of engagement with terrorists everywhere. Nothing but a strong stand will do. That will not always be popular, as we have seen in Spain, regardless of whether the enemy is al Qaeda, Moqtada al-Sadr or the IRA. Critics of President [George W.] Bush charge that he has squandered the worldwide sympathy for the U.S. that obtained in the immediate aftermath of the Twin Towers attack; but there never was a golden age.

Let me give the example from Ireland, a European country with familial ties to America. After 9/11, the newspaper of the fastest-growing political party in Ireland, Sinn Fein, editorialized that the U.S. had effectively brought the attack upon itself through its "imperialist" foreign policy. Irish public opinion was massively against even the war in Afghanistan. The notion that a more sensitive, conscience-stricken U.S. policy would generate more support in international councils is a delusion.

Unless terrorism has visited your door and murdered your citizens, you do not fully grasp its enormity, its evil, and the necessity to defeat it.

Success requires perseverance. It took a quarter of a century, but the British state and the local majority stayed the course in Northern Ireland. A humiliating withdrawal from Iraq with the job only half completed would be a shot in the arm for terrorists world-wide. Pretending that the war against terrorism can be won quickly is as illusory as pretending that a recalibration of U.S. policy toward Israel will deliver a coup de grace against all the violent forms of Islam that threaten our interests.

The reality is that in much of Western Europe the potential threat from GM [genetically modified] foods and juvenile obesity exercise the minds of politicians more than the threat from revolutionary Islam. As a former First Minister of Northern Ireland, I know that unless terrorism has visited your door and murdered your citizens, you do not fully grasp its enormity, its evil, and the necessity to defeat it. The truth is that the battle against terror is not only hard, but lonely.

5

The United States Should Negotiate with North Korea

Selig S. Harrison

Selig S. Harrison is the director of the Asia Program at the Center for International Policy. He is the author of six books, including Korean Endgame: A Strategy for Reunification and U.S. Disengagement.

After rejecting the vague security guarantee offered by the United States, South Korea, and Japan in December 2003, North Korea issued a counterproposal that included halting its plutonium program. U.S. president George W. Bush refused this offer, saying the United States will not resume talks until North Korea dismantles its entire nuclear program. In my numerous discussions with North Korean officials, it has become clear that, contrary to its image, North Korea is divided into two camps: those who favor nuclear weapons over reconciling with the United States, and those who are willing to dismantle their nuclear arsenal in exchange for better relations with the United States. The United States should offer encouragement to the latter group by leaving aside its pursuit of regime change in exchange for a program to dismantle North Korea's nuclear program. When negotiations resume, the United States should offer a more specific security guarantee and economic aid to North Korea in return for its concessions.

Selig S. Harrison, "N. Korean 'Good Guys' Require U.S. Assistance," *USA Today*, January 7, 2004. Copyright © 2004, USA Today. Reproduced by permission of the author.

In *The Third World War*, a thriller by British journalist Humphrey Hawksley, the United States and North Korea angrily break off negotiations on [North Korean capital] Pyongyang's nuclear weapons program. When North Korean leader Kim Jong Il then makes a conciliatory offer—promptly spurned by Washington—a hard-line general seizes power, denounces Kim for "appeasement" and begins plotting with anti-U.S. Islamic terrorist groups centered in Pakistan. North Korea fires a missile at a U.S. base in Japan, Tokyo retaliates with nuclear weapons, and Pakistan launches simultaneous attacks on India that draw Russia, China and the United States into a global holocaust.

A wildly improbable scenario? Not entirely. It correctly depicts Kim as the lesser of evils in North Korea and sharply underlines what's wrong with American policy toward Pyongyang.

Plans to hold a new round of negotiations with North Korea are stalled because the [George W.] Bush administration is offering vaguely defined terms for a settlement that ignore the ongoing policy struggle in Pyongyang. This week [January 2004], a private U.S. delegation is visiting North Korea to discuss its nuclear weapons program. But Bush officials were cool to the visit, saying a six-nation effort is the correct way to pursue negotiations. Protracted diplomatic bargaining now lies ahead, which will determine whether Washington, Pyongyang and their negotiating partners (China, Russia, Japan and South Korea) move toward a settlement or deadlock with incalculable consequences.

Last month [December 2003], the U.S., South Korea and Japan offered North Korea a proposed security guarantee containing only a broad pledge to maintain the "peace and stability" of the Korean peninsula. Pyongyang, which wants those nations to promise not to attack North Korea or seek regime change, rejected that. Instead, it offered to start negotiations by freezing its plutonium program in exchange for U.S. economic aid, the resumption of oil shipments and its removal from the U.S. list of terrorist states. President Bush, in turn, rejected that offer, insisting that North Korea dismantle, not just freeze, its entire nuclear program before dialogue can begin on other issues. On Tuesday [January 6, 2004], North Korea fine-tuned its offer, adding a specific pledge to bar nuclear tests, but again stopped short of Bush's precondition.

The United States should help the "good guys" win by abandoning its regime-change hopes.

Two Camps

During my seven visits to North Korea since 1972, I have had increasingly frank exchanges with many officials, often informally over dinner. In contrast with its monolithic image, the country is divided into two camps: hard-liners who favor nuclear weapons and believe reconciling with the U.S. is impossible, and pragmatists ready to dismantle their nuclear weapons program in return for security guarantees, U.S. recognition and economic assistance.

The United States should help the "good guys" win by abandoning its regime-change hopes and pursuing a verifiable, step-by-step process of dismantling North Korea's nuclear capability, with economic rewards along the way.

Kim Jong Il does not have the absolute control that his late father, Kim Il Sung, had. Therefore, although he sides with the pragmatists, he cannot get hard-liners to go along with a nuclear settlement without tangible benefits and an overall shift in U.S. policy toward coexistence.

One way to help the good guys is to cool down the rhetoric. Bush has said he "loathes" Kim Jong Il and wants to "topple" his dictatorship. But the only way to prevent North Korea from selling bomb-making plutonium to terrorists is to deal with Kim, not threaten him. He is a cunning opportunist, ready to give up his nuclear weapons program if that is the best way to bolster his regime economically and stabilize his power. Policies designed to destabilize his regime will only strengthen the hard-liners. To soften Kim's dictatorship and promote democratization, the U.S. should encourage his current economic reforms though a broad normalization of relations, which would help open up the country.

Both North Korea and the U.S. have relaxed their positions slightly. North Korea made the first move with a little-noticed offer on Aug. 27 [2003], now repeated, to put its plutonium stockpile under verifiable controls. Until three months ago [October 2003], the Bush administration insisted that North Korea dismantle its nuclear-weapons effort all at once as a precondition for dialogue on other issues, including its key demand for a U.S. security guarantee. Then, on his October [2003] Asian trip, Bush signaled his readiness to "consider" a six-nation northeast Asian security pledge. However, the administration has yet to resolve internal conflicts over the type of security guarantee.

The United States should agree to a security guarantee that would remain in effect while negotiations proceed.

One Step at a Time

When talks resume, the United States should agree to a security guarantee that would remain in effect while negotiations proceed and would become permanent only upon the satisfactory conclusion of the step-by-step process. At each step, North Korea would get economic rewards in return for its concessions and steadily increasing U.S. inspection access.

North Korea is not likely to give up its nuclear weapons program until the White House persuades Pyongyang that it is no longer seeking to topple the Kim regime. This was the message conveyed by Jo Sung Ju, American affairs director in the foreign ministry, and three other visiting North Korean officials during a two-day dialogue with six Americans in mid-November [2003] in which I participated.

Repeatedly, the North Korean delegates emphasized that "coexistence" is the key to resolving the nuclear crisis. What North Korea wants, they said, is a security guarantee that would not only revoke the threat of a U.S. pre-emptive attack, but also would pledge to "respect the sovereignty" of North Korea by abandoning the often-stated goal of "regime change."

"Why would we need nuclear weapons if we no longer feel threatened?" asked one. "Why would we give up our right to have them if you keep talking about regime change? It's as simple as that."

Negotiating with North Korea Has Encouraged Its Negative Actions

Stephen Rademaker

Stephen Rademaker has been the acting assistant secretary for the Bureau of International Security and Nonproliferation at the U.S. Department of State since 2005. He has held positions on the House of Representatives Committee on International Relations and Select Committee on Homeland Security.

North Korean leader Kim Jong-il fulfilled his promise to shut down the nuclear reactor at Yongbyon, and a summit between the leader of South Korea and him was held in August 2007. While this is good news, it would be unwise to expect a permanent diplomatic resolution to North Korea's nuclear stand-off. Time and time again in the past fifteen years, the international community has rewarded North Korea for bad behavior. As a recent example, North Korea agreed to a 2007 De-nuclearization Action Plan in which it promised to freeze its nuclear facilities at Yongbyon and engage in an energy dialogue with the United States. North Korea was paid generously in fuel for this agreement and even so, refused to go forward with talks until it was given a substantial sum of money. North Korea has clearly learned from this pattern of response from the international community that when it violates agreements, it will be threatened but ultimately given attractive incentives to sign future agreements, by which it may or may not abide.

Stephen Rademaker, "Why North Korea Continues to Defy the World," *Financial Times*, August 13, 2007, p. 9. Copyright © 2007 Stephen G. Rademaker. Reproduced by permission.

Most of the recent diplomatic news on North Korea is encouraging. After protracted delays, Kim Jong-il last month [July 2007] honoured the promise he made in February [2007] to shut down his nuclear reactor at Yongbyon. This paved the way for the announcement last week [August 2007] of the first summit between leaders of the two Koreas in seven years. It will be held this month [August 2007].

The summit almost certainly will result in warmer relations between Seoul and Pyongyang. North Korea undoubtedly expects material benefits as well. After the last summit in 2000, it emerged that North Korea had successfully demanded the transfer of hundreds of millions of dollars in cash as a precondition to participating. South Korea has made clear that no money will change hands this time, but North Korea certainly does not expect to leave the meeting empty-handed.

The closure of Yongbyon has also led to resumption of the six- party talks on nuclear disarmament. But no matter what incremental progress is made in coming months, it would defy experience to believe that a permanent diplomatic resolution to the nuclear stand-off is at hand. After 15 years of negotiations over its nuclear programme, the main lesson North Korea has drawn is that obstruction, delay and non-compliance will elicit additional concessions. It therefore must be expected to obstruct, delay and not comply.

The international community never set out to reward North Korea for bad behaviour, but over the past 15 years that is precisely what it has done. In 1993 North Korea triggered an international crisis by announcing its withdrawal from the Nuclear Nonproliferation Treaty (NPT). Its reward was the [1994] Agreed Framework. Under that agreement, North Korea took back its withdrawal from the NPT and committed to freeze and eventually dismantle its plutonium-based nuclear weapons programme. In exchange, North Korea was promised two light water nuclear reactors worth about [4.5 billion] dollars plus 500,000 tons of fuel oil each year.

Upping the Ante

North Korea liked this bargain so much that it decided to set up a parallel, uranium-based nuclear weapons programme to see what price it might fetch. The [George W.] Bush administration suspended implementation of the Agreed Framework over this violation in 2002, so again the North Koreans upped the ante. First, they again announced their withdrawal from the NPT. When that did not work, they geared up their nuclear weapons programme, testing a nuclear weapon in October 2006.

Despite years of warnings to North Korea . . . the principal consequence of the [nuclear weapons] test was to jump-start negotiations.

Despite years of warnings to North Korea that a nuclear weapons test would cross a "red line", the principal consequence of the test was to jump-start negotiations. By February 2007, agreement was reached on a Denuclearisation Action Plan. Under this agreement, North Korea again promised to freeze its nuclear facilities at Yongbyon. In exchange, it was promised 1 m[illion] tons of fuel oil, plus the initiation of an energy dialogue in which the US has promised "to discuss, at an appropriate time, the subject of the provision of light water reactor (sic) to (North Korea)".

No sooner was this agreed than North Korea threw on the brakes, refusing to do anything until it received [25 million] dollars that had been frozen in a Macao bank. The Bush administration acquiesced in order to preserve the February agreement, even though that agreement contained no such precondition and the administration had long insisted that the issues were unrelated. Notwithstanding that the US Treasury considered the funds in question so dirty that it had sought to shut down the Macao bank that held them, the Federal Reserve Bank of New York ultimately was enlisted to transfer the funds back to North Korea.

Muted Response to Latest Tests

Meanwhile, two UN Security Council resolutions adopted in 2006 immediately following North Korean weapons tests have been shelved. These resolutions had required more responsible behaviour by North Korea and imposed limited international sanctions. A late-June missile test by North Korea in plain violation of the resolutions elicited barely a whisper of protest.

Having got its way on the frozen funds and on implementation of the Security Council resolutions, North Korea is sure to make additional demands. It has already said it will take no further steps to implement the February agreement until the US ends the trade embargo and removes it from the US list of terrorism sponsors.

Assuming they receive satisfaction on these issues, two much more serious sticking points can be expected to emerge. First, they will not want to reveal the full extent of their nuclear weapons programme—most importantly their uranium enrichment activities—as required under the February agreement. Second, they will make further progress conditional on the resumption of the [4.5 billion] dollars light water reactor project begun during the [Bill] Clinton administration.

It is safe to assume that diplomacy is unlikely to end the North Korean nuclear weapons threat for the foreseeable future.

What We Can Expect

If the North Koreans can prevail on both issues, they effectively will have reinstated the Agreed Framework—except that now they have additional nuclear weapons, have tested them, and will have been given a pass on their uranium enrichment programme. And, as under the Agreed Framework, they will insist that we do not get what we want—dismantlement of their nuclear weapons and related infrastructure—until construction of the light water reactors is complete. This will afford them another decade during which to present additional demands.

Alternatively, if the North Koreans do not prevail on both issues, they will put the diplomatic process on indefinite hold. Then, at a propitious moment, they will plunge it into another crisis to bully others into meeting their demands.

Either way, it is safe to assume that diplomacy is unlikely to end the North Korean nuclear weapons threat for the foreseeable future.

7

Israel Should Negotiate with Hamas

Johann Hari

Johann Hari is a journalist whose work has appeared in the New York Times, Los Angeles Times, Guardian, Le Monde, and numerous other publications. He has written a twice-weekly column for the London-based Independent *since 2003.*

A protest by primarily Palestinian women in September 2007 demonstrated the true desire for peace among the majority of Palestinians. In fact, two polls show that Palestinians are generally more pro-peace than Israelis. Fighting between Palestinian factions like Fatah and Hamas illustrates the inevitable result of putting enormous pressure on a group of people, as the Israeli government has done to the Palestinians in retribution for electing a Hamas-led government. Yet the election should not be a surprise since the Palestinians have hardly been rewarded for electing moderates in the past. Since being elected, Hamas has actually behaved in a diplomatic fashion, only to be met by sanctions from the United States and Israel. Israel may be doing this in hopes of wearing down the will of the Palestinians; worse, it may be intentionally sabotaging potential partners in peace. The only way to solve the current crisis is for Israel to negotiate with Hamas, which is offering a long-term ceasefire. Unfortunately, it appears that Israel will reject this opportunity.

Johann Hari, "Israel Must Negotiate with Hamas," *The Independent*, June 18, 2007. Copyright © 2007 Independent Newspapers (UK) Ltd. Reproduced by permission.

The enemies of the Palestinian people have been presenting the political chaos of the [June 2007] as evidence that they are premodern savages, capable only of building a Mogadishu [war-ravaged Somalian capital] on the Mediterranean. But [in June 2007], the real voice of the Palestinian people echoed out, for a fleeting moment.

Thousands of protesters—mostly women—took to the streets. They called not for sharia law or Qassam rockets against Israeli cities, but for peace. Amal Hellis, a 35-year-old mother-of-two, said: "I am not afraid. I will die to save my family and to save Palestine." Her eldest son Medhat is a member of Fatah; her youngest son Refaat belongs to Hamas. When the marchers reached the Al Ghifary tower near the beachfront, they were fired on by gunmen—but they did not run away. The old women and their granddaughters stood in the crossfire, waving Palestinian flags and singing "Give Peace a Chance".

Hamas gunmen fired from above; Fatah fighters threatened them on the ground. The women surrounded the Fatah man, forcing him with nothing but plain moral pressure to lower his rifle. Only when one of the protesters was caught in the chest by a sniper did they finally disperse.

These protesters speak for a majority of Palestinians. In the most recent poll of them conducted by the Palestinian Centre for Policy and Survey Research, 63 per cent supported full recognition of Israel in return for a proper Palestinian state. These supporters of a negotiated peace include, crucially, a majority of Hamas supporters.

This means there is actually a bigger pro-peace constituency in Palestine than in Israel, where Hebrew newspaper *Yediot Aharanot* polling just found that 58 per cent of Israelis now reject the idea of trading land for peace, because they think the Palestinians are irrevocably committed to destroying them.

Fighting Is a Result of Circumstance

The current crackle of war is not evidence that the Palestinians are incapable of self-government. It is evidence of what happens to human beings when they are rammed into a pressure cooker and the temperature is slowly ramped up.

In [such as the Palestinian] situation, any people, anywhere, would begin to turn on each other.

When I was last in Gaza a few months ago, the borders of Palestine had been hermetically sealed by the world for months as punishment for choosing Hamas in a free election. One-and-a-half million people were locked into a tiny space no bigger than the Isle of Wight [about 147 sq. miles]. Nothing went in; nothing went out. The hospitals were on the brink of collapse because if a piece of equipment broke they could not get new parts. Almost everyone was out of work because they couldn't sell to the world a few miles away.

In this situation, any people, anywhere, would begin to turn on each other. As the Palestinian foreign minister Ziad Abu Amr puts it: "If you have two brothers put into a cage and deprive them of the basic essential needs for life, they will fight."

On top of this, the outside world has actually discouraged and humiliated the Palestinian moderates. When he took charge in 2005, the Fatah President Mahmoud Abbas made it plain he would offer huge compromises to Israel in return for a state. [Israeli prime minister] Ariel Sharon offered him a few lifted roadblocks in return. The message to the Palestinians was clear: electing pragmatists will get you nothing. So the next year, in desperation they elected Hamas, an Islamic fundamentalist organisation whose constitution includes statements from the anti-Semitic forgery, the Protocols of the Elders of Zion.

No Reward for Diplomacy

Regular readers [of the *Independent*] will know that I loathe Hamas, but I have to acknowledge that, upon election, their leaders undeniably behaved in a pragmatic way. They did not start introducing the savagery of sharia law, or oppressing women. Instead, they observed the unilateral truce with Israel. They offered a hudna (ceasefire) that would last a generation. They gave up staging suicide-murders against Israeli civilians. They even said they would respect all previous agreements signed by the Palestinian Authority—a de facto concession that they would recognise Israel.

And in return? They received nothing but abuse and a determined attempt to dislodge them from power, by boycott and, more slowly, by bullet. The US and Israel began arming an especially authoritarian wing of Fatah, headed by Mohammed Dahlan, with the plain intention of him toppling Hamas sooner or later. The Washington-based architect of this policy is Deputy National Security Advisor Elliot Abrams, a man who in the 1980s secretly armed the openly fascist Contra militias in an attempt to topple the Sandinista government in Nicaragua. By denying Hamas power through a legitimate election, and arming their enemies for a future liquidation, the US and Israel virtually guaranteed Hamas would seize power.

Why is the Israeli government doing this? There are a range of possible explanations. One, associated with former Prime Minister Bibi Netanyahu and current Deputy Prime Minister Avigdor Lieberman, is the belief that the Palestinians will only compromise once they have been totally defeated by overwhelming force. They reckon that if the Palestinians are throttled for long enough, sooner or later they will cower, beg for mercy, and accept Israeli terms.

The next, and more disturbing, explanation is that the Israeli government may be deliberately thwarting potential peace partners. Uri Avnery, a former member of the Israeli Knesset [parliament] and disillusioned Irgun [Zionist extremist group] fighter, explains why: "There has always been a tendency in Israel to prefer expansion and settlement to compromise and peace. Our government has worked for years to destroy Fatah, in order to avoid the need to negotiate an agreement that would inevitably lead to the withdrawal of the settlements from Palestinian land. Now, when it seems this aim has been achieved, they have no idea what to do about the Hamas victory."

There is still a way out of this. Israel must negotiate with Hamas.

The Only Option

There is still a way out of this. Israel must negotiate with Hamas. They are offering a long, long ceasefire. The Arab states are even—in a startling offer from Saudi Arabia—offering full recognition and normalisation of Israel in the region, if only Israel returns to its legal borders. Perhaps they are lying. Perhaps it is a trick. But it is the only game-plan in town that offers even the chance of a happy ending.

But Israel seems determined not to take this chance. Ehud Barak, the ex-PM [prime minister] back as Defence Minister, is briefing that he will bomb Gaza yet again, and within weeks. He is proposing to actually intensify the blockade of the Gaza Strip for a few weeks, to "pressure" Hamas.

The Israeli government is clinging to the belief that the harder you beat the Palestinians, the softer their leaders will become. This mentality created the current collapse. It will only drag the Middle East further and further away from the sane voices of women such as Amal Hellis, singing songs of peace.

8

Israel Should Not Negotiate with the Palestinians

Michael Rubin

Michael Rubin is a resident scholar at the American Enterprise Institute and editor of Middle East Quarterly. *He is also a former political adviser to the Coalition Provisional Authority in Iraq.*

Israel's attacks on Lebanon have been widely decried by Western governments who say that diplomacy is more effective at achieving peace than retaliation. History does not support this assertion. The United States has consistently rewarded noncompliance from terrorist leaders, while rejecting retaliatory violence. This has made the United States weak in the eyes of terrorists, who specifically target Americans as a result. Contrary to American sentiment, using disproportionate violence to respond to terrorism is often the most effective response. A peace that is lasting is rarely achieved between equals; rather, it is usually achieved between a strong power and a weak power, as seen with the U.S. bombing of Japan that ended World War II. Diplomacy that rewards terrorists actually brings more violence. Diplomacy in the Middle East must only come after Hezbollah and Hamas are eliminated.

As bombs continue to drop on Lebanon and rockets on Israel, the West has begun to lose its resolve. On July 14 [2006], French president Jacques Chirac condemned Israel's military action as "completely disproportionate." Russian Presi-

Michael Rubin, "Eradication First: Before Diplomacy," *National Review Online*, July 17, 2006. Reproduced by permission.

dent Vladimir Putin called Israel's "use of full-scale force" unacceptable. While President George W. Bush stood firm in his moral clarity, the State Department was more cautious. "It is extremely important that Israel exercise restraint in its acts of self defense," [secretary of state] Condoleezza Rice told reporters on July 13 [2006].

Some U.S. politicians sought to capitalize on the latest violence for political gain. Senator Hillary Clinton blamed the Bush administration for the outburst of violence. "We've had five and a half years of a failed experiment in tough talk absent diplomacy and engagement. I think it's time to go back to what works, and what has historically worked and what can work again."

Clinton should go back and reread her history. Premature recourse to diplomacy backfires. [Former U.S. president] Bill Clinton's diplomatic efforts were well-intentioned but they resulted not in peace, but in a far more violent conflict. The fault for this does not lie with Clinton, but rather with an Iranian and Arab leadership that had not abandoned violence as a mechanism to achieve their goals.

Still, the Clinton administration trusted [Palestinian leader Yasser] Arafat as a partner far longer than the evidence warranted. They were not alone. Often in Washington, politicians become so wedded to the success of their policy initiatives, that they ignore the reality of its failure.

The Bush administration was not as willing to accept Yasser Arafat's duplicity. While in December 2001, Secretary of State Colin Powell held out hope that Arafat's call to end armed struggle against Israel was sincere, his decision to withhold judgment was wise. As Arafat won European praise for his ceasefire, Iranian and Hezbollah [Islamic militant organization based in Lebanon] officials were loading 50 tons of weaponry onto the *Karine-A* [freighter], destination: Gaza. Throughout the intifada [Palestinian violent uprising] Arafat's diplomacy was insincere. He, like other terrorists and rogue leaders, ran to diplomats and the United Nations when he feared retaliation, the playground equivalent of sucker-punching a classmate when the teacher's back is turned, and then crying for intercession as the victim fights back.

The Solution Was Not Diplomacy

Arafat and many Hamas [Palestinian Islamic militant organization and political party] leaders paid the price for their strategy: It was not diplomacy which ended the intifada. Rather, the U.S. and Israeli quarantine of Arafat and Israel's targeted assassination campaign against other terrorist leaders created accountability and broke the back of the terrorist campaign.

It was at this point, though, that both [Israeli prime minister] Ariel Sharon and George Bush snatched defeat from the jaws of victory. Politicians should never reward violence and non-compliance. The second intifada which followed then—Israeli Prime Minister Ehud Barak's May 2000 withdrawal from southern Lebanon made the violence which engulfed Gaza after Sharon's unilateral disengagement predictable. Bush's mistake was rewarding Iran's noncompliance. Just days after he reversed his policy and rewarded Iran, [the] Iranian Supreme Leader ridiculed U.S. weakness. "In Iraq, you failed. You say you have spent 300 billion dollars to bring a government in office that obeys you. But it did not happen. In Palestine, you made all attempts to prevent Hamas from coming to power and again you failed. Why don't you admit that you are weak and your razor is blunt?" he declared on June 4, 2006.

The problem with the West's policy in the Middle East is ... [its] failure to allow retaliatory violence and impose accountability.

The problem with the West's policy in the Middle East is not lack of diplomacy, but rather failure to allow retaliatory violence and impose accountability. During the Clinton years, terrorists believed they could strike U.S. interests with near impunity. In 1996, Clinton failed to respond to Iranian planning, training, and supplying for the terrorists which struck the Khobar towers [in Saudi Arabia]. In 1998, U.S. retaliation in response to al Qaeda's East Africa embassy bombings was weakwristed, and in 2000, the response to the U.S.S. *Cole* bombing was nonexistent. Israel too suffered from an erosion of its deterrence.

Disproportionate Force Can Bring Peace

Not only is vengeance against terrorism sometimes necessary, but it is more likely to bring peace if it is disproportionate. The Bush administration's response to the 9/11 terrorist attacks was not to bring down a couple buildings in Kabul or Qandahar [in Afghanistan], nor shoot missiles at empty buildings or training camps, but rather to launch war on al Qaeda and bring the Taliban government to its knees.

For the West, moral equivalency is also a handicap. True, terrorists may also argue that the way to alter Western policy is through violence. But that is all the more reason why the West must ensure its own victory first.

When academics and commentators decry disproportionate force as an obstacle to peace, they replace analysis with platitudes. Lasting peace is seldom made between equals, but rather between strong and weak. The United States ended World War II precisely because it was willing to use disproportionate force. In doing so, it allowed Japan to rebuild and thrive. England and France did not pull back from Germany and allow the Nazi regime to re-arm and try again. Wars are fought until they are won. Among Israel's neighbors, only Egypt and Jordan have accepted peace with the Jewish state. In 1977, Egyptian president Anwar Sadat sought peace only after a disastrous attempt at war. King Hussein of Jordan also accepted peace—not as formally at first—after understanding the price of war. Negotiations between Jerusalem, Cairo, and Amman succeeded because they accepted that violence could not achieve their aims, an epiphany still lost upon many in the Arab world and Iran. The irony of the [1993] Oslo Accords was that those that fought the first intifada were not those handed the reins of leadership. Both U.S. and Israeli leaders enabled the Tunisia-based faction of the Palestine Liberation Organization to take control. Arafat viewed his chairmanship over the Palestinian Authority as an entitlement, without understanding his responsibility.

That anyone would intercede to enable someone whose goal is genocide to continue is irresponsible, if not hateful.

Diplomacy Can Spur More Violence

Diplomacy that preserves a status quo in which terrorists win concession through violence ensures future bloodshed. Hezbollah is not a movement whose existence diplomats should intercede to preserve. While world leaders condemned Iranian president Mahmud Ahmadinejad's Holocaust denial and threats to eradicate Israel from the map, they ignore that on April 9, 2000, Hezbollah leader Hassan Nasrallah declared, "The Jews invented the legend of the Nazi atrocities," and argued, "Anyone who reads the Koran and the holy writings of the monotheistic religions sees what they did to the prophets, and what acts of madness and slaughter the Jews carried out throughout history. . . . Anyone who reads these texts cannot think of co-existence with them, of peace with them, or about accepting their presence, not only in Palestine of 1948 but even in a small village in Palestine, because they are a cancer which is liable to spread again at any moment." Nasrallah has made his aims clear. That anyone would intercede to enable someone whose goal is genocide to continue is irresponsible, if not hateful. Nasrallah later provided an answer to those progressives tempted to argue the problem to be Israel's existence. To the Hezbollah leader, Israel is just one part of the fight. On October 22, 2002, Hassan Nasrallah told Lebanon's *Daily Star*, "If they [the Jews] all gather in Israel, it will save us the trouble of going after them world wide."

There will be a role for diplomacy in the Middle East, but it will only be successful if it commences after the eradication of both Hezbollah and Hamas, and after their paymasters pay a terrible cost for their support. This does not mean that Israel is without blame. Lebanese politicians may have been cowardly in their failure to exert sovereignty following Israel's May 2000 withdrawal from southern Lebanon. The State Department and European foreign ministries were negligent in their failure to keep up the pressure on Hezbollah, Damascus, and Tehran following the Cedar Revolution [a series of protests in Lebanon in response to the assassination of former prime minister Rafik Hariri]. But there will never be peace if Syria and Iran are allowed to use Lebanon as a proxy battlefield safe and secure in the knowledge that they will not pay directly. If peace is the aim, it is imperative to punish the Syrian and Iranian leadership. Most Lebanese are victims, too.

9

Israel's Refusal to Negotiate with Palestine Has Led to More Terrorism

Marc Gopin

Marc Gopin is the director of the Center on Religion, Diplomacy, and Conflict Resolution at George Mason University in Virginia. He is the author of several books, including Holy War, Holy Peace.

By refusing to negotiate with moderate Palestinian leaders, former Israeli prime minister Ariel Sharon drove the Palestinian people into the radical hands of Hamas. The results have been bad for both sides: Israel has been forced to give up its territory in Gaza, and the Palestinian people have lost their moderate leadership. If Israel had agreed to hold talks with Palestinian leaders in the first place, world leaders would have understood the growing frustration of average Palestinians that led to the election of Hamas, perhaps preventing that election. At this point, instead of waiting for the United States to lead diplomatic negotiations, Israel needs to sit down with Palestinian leaders and begin a new peace process.

Israel's former prime minister Ariel Sharon could never bring himself to sit across from an equal Palestinian partner. As a result, Israel lost an opportunity to gain, in return for giving back Gaza [the Gaza Strip, which Israel relinquished to the Palestinians in 2005], serious changes in the Palestinians'

Marc Gopin, "A Failure to Communicate," *The Christian Century*, vol. 123, May 30, 2006, pp. 8–9. Copyright © 2006 by The Christian Century Foundation. All rights reserved. Reproduced by permission.

approach to their struggle. It turned out that Sharon gave Gaza not to the Palestinian people but to Hamas [Palestinian Islamist militant organization, elected in 2006 as the government of the Palestinian people]. History will judge this as a free favor to Arab radicalism.

Israel's unilateral pullout from Gaza was judged by the Palestinians and much of the Arab world as an Israeli acknowledgment that it had lost control of Gaza to Hamas, and therefore it was seen as a victory for suicide terrorism. It was also a stunning rebuke of Palestinian moderates, since no other Palestinian leader has been as moderate as Prime Minister Mahmoud Abbas, and he was ignored by the Israelis in the Gaza pullout.

Hamas has become stronger because of the steady corruption and deterioration of the Palestinian [National] Authority [governmental organization that controls security and civilian issues in urban Palestinian areas and civilian issues in rural Palestinian areas]. For that there is blame to go around, including some for the Palestinian elites. But if the Israelis had shown a willingness to engage seriously with moderate Palestinian demands, they might not be facing a Hamas government right now.

Some observers believe that dominance by Palestinian radicals was always the goal of the Israeli right, since reaching the conclusion that "there is no partner" on the Palestinian side would give Israel permission to extend control over greater and greater swaths of the West Bank [territory on the west bank of the Jordan River]. The irony is that now everyone has lost: the Israeli right is losing more territory as the government plans more unilateral pullouts, and the Palestinians have lost moderate leadership. On balance, this still benefits Israeli unilateralism, because Israel is securing the most coveted of the contested areas in and around Jerusalem.

Some Progress

Sharonism, the Gaza pullout, and the birth of Kadima, the new Israeli centrist party, are expressions of an evolution in internal Israeli thinking, just as the political victory—at least for now—of Hamas is an expression of an internal evolution of Palestinian thinking in response to corruption and lack of progress. Taken by themselves, these are healthy evolutions.

Israeli civil society is on a more stable, centrist course than it has been in many years. The vision of some Israelis of a Greater Israel—with no Palestinian state or with Palestinians being transferred out of Israel—was so utterly at odds with a vision of a democratic Israel that there was serious danger of civil conflict. That is abating. But there is no vision of peace to take its place other than a unilateral divorce from the Palestinians.

Similarly, corruption and its divisive threat to the future of Palestine is going to be ameliorated by Hamas, although we do not know yet whether the political construction of the Palestinian Authority will be democratic or will involve the imposition of shari'a law [a legal framework based on Muslim principles].

There is no peace without conversation, secret or public.

The problem is that neither one of these developments evolved in conversation with the enemy next door. There is no peace without conversation, secret or public, nor will there be realistic internal debate that will yield peace or coexistence with enemies. If a conversation had been ongoing, Israelis would have understood how wrong it was to go through the trauma of a pullout without the benefit of strengthening Palestinian moderates and peacemakers, and they would have figured out a scheme, together with moderate Palestinians, to reap those benefits. If the conversations had been ongoing, the world would have understood how fed up average Palestinians were with corruptions imposed on them, and it would have stopped feeding the corruption rather than make Hamas the most attractive game in town.

What Should Have Happened

Now the conversation is stuck. Americans and Israelis have good reason to thwart public support for Hamas until it renounces terrorism. But U.S. leaders never should have touted "democratization" as an answer when that meant elections that would lead to the rise of antidemocratic parties.

Rather than promote elections, the U.S. should have insisted on promoting the foundations of democracy. It should have listened to the Arab masses who are clamoring mostly for jobs and a fair share of wealth. They should have pushed for basic Palestinian humanitarian needs and human rights as a way of making peace more attractive.

The U.S. is never going to make Israel safer in the Middle East.

If they wanted elections, U.S. leaders should have insisted, through negotiations, on no less from Hamas than was asked of Sinn Fein [the political arm of the Irish Republican Army] in Northern Ireland—renunciation of violence and the giving-up of weapons. None of that clarity was to be found, or there was no U.S. negotiator like George Mitchell [former U.S. special envoy to Northern Ireland] involved in conversation. There have been no serious U.S negotiations with Palestinians for years, because [the George W. Bush] White House has been a master at global alienation, unilateralism, arrogance, and self-fulfilling prophecies of military confrontation and conquest.

It is time for Israel's political establishment to stop looking to the Pentagon for inspiration. The U.S. is never going to make Israel safer in the Middle East. Only Israel has that capacity, together with the Palestinians as equal partners.

Oslo II?

The Oslo peace process [which resulted in the Oslo Peace Accords in 1993] of decades ago was a brilliant effort to bring together moderate Israelis and Palestinians, to design a future together. It was flawed in that it failed to include essential constituencies on both sides—religious communities and their militants. Whatever their methods and anti-democratic predilections, Jewish and Muslim radicals had important needs and demands that were virtually eliminated from serious discussion—issues surrounding holy land, holy places, historical claims, lifestyles in any future states and so forth. Had their interests and needs been at least part of the bargaining, we might have avoided the failure of the peace process.

The time has come for Oslo II, with the key players in Israel and Palestine acting this time without the arrogance of secular elites who do not pay attention to the poor and the religious on both sides. There is only one choice for the future: conversation, conversation and conversation, so that the moves made on each side may create a road back to the peace process.

10

Israel and the United States Should Negotiate with Syria

Gidon D. Remba

Gidon D. Remba is national executive director of Ameinu: Liberal Values, Progressive Israel and a cofounder of Chicago Peace Now. He writes a column on Israel and the Middle East for the Jewish Chronicle *in Pittsburgh.*

Soon after the Lebanese cease-fire took effect, Israel's defense minister, Amir Peretz, proposed holding peace talks with Syria. Many criticized Peretz's move, saying it illustrated his lack of security experience. Yet several other Israeli officials, including those with hawkish tendencies like Avi Dichter, agreed that it was time to begin discussions with Syria. Indeed, this is the ideal time to give Syria a political incentive to cut off ties with Hezbollah and Hamas and align itself, instead, with the West. The United States successfully used this tactic to lure Egypt away from the Soviets and into an alliance with the United States and a treaty with Israel. The current situation offers a unique opportunity to test the true intentions of the Syrians and give them a chance to abandon their terrorist affiliations.

No sooner had the Lebanon cease-fire taken hold when Israeli Defense Minister Amir Peretz proposed peace talks with Syria. The critics pounced on him forthwith: The novice minister, notorious for his lack of security experience, "jumped the gun," showing that he had as much to learn about the art of diplomacy as he did about the art of war.

Gidon D. Remba, "Now May Be the Time to Pry Syria from Terrorist Camp," *The Jewish Chronicle*, September 7, 2006, p. 6. Copyright © 2006 Gidon D. Remba. Reproduced by permission.

But was it Peretz' want of diplomatic and security credentials that accounted for the novitiate minister's call for talks with Syria?

Soon after Peretz spoke, Avi Dichter, Israel's hawkish internal security minister and former chief of the Shin Bet [Israel's internal security agency], opined: "In exchange for peace with Syria, Israel can leave the Golan Heights, [returning] to the international border. We have paid similar territorial prices for peace with Jordan and Egypt."

"A process of discussions with Syria is legitimate—and very suitable," he went on. "Israel can initiate it. Ultimately, initiatives of this kind are [conducted by] a third party—and there is an abundance of third parties in the world. If a third party approaches us, we must reply in the affirmative. Any political process is preferable to a military-fighting process, be it with Syria or with Lebanon."

Echoing Peretz, Foreign Minister Tzipi Livni suddenly appointed Ya'akov Dayan as a special "project manager" for possible negotiations with Syria. Dayan wasted no time meeting with officials who headed Israel's Syrian negotiations team under Prime Ministers Yitzhak Rabin and Ehud Barak in the mid- and late-1990s. Dayan has been tasked with presenting Livni "with a document detailing the chances for resuming the diplomatic dialogue with Syria in light of Syrian and Israeli positions on borders, security and normalization," reported Ha'aretz [Israeli daily newspaper]. Knesset [Israel's legislature] Member Danny Yatom, a former Mossad [Israel's intelligence agency] director and chief of the IDF's [Israel Defense Force, Israel's military forces] Central Command, has been among those in the Labor Party calling for engagement with Syria.

The Right Conditions

Prime Minister [Ehud] Olmert, portrayed by some as having slapped down any diplomatic exchange with Syria, actually left the door ajar: "I will negotiate only when Syria undergoes

fundamental change with regard to its open support for terrorism." If Syria stopped aiding Hezbollah and Hamas, Olmert
was indicating Israel's readiness to resume the peace talks
aborted in 2000. Now Peretz has again urged that Israel "do
everything possible to create the conditions for a dialogue
with the Palestinians and on the Syrian front as well."

Were Peretz's remarks the musings of a dilettante? If so, he
was in illustrious company. Were Peretz, Dichter, Olmert and
Livni's moves nothing more than the uncoordinated ram-
blings of unruly and irresponsible ministers? Or did they re-
flect a recognition among many in the Israeli government that
the strategic benefits for Israel of a resumption of talks with
Syria could be unparalleled?

---

*Offer Syria a potent political incentive to dry up
Hezbollah's weapons flow.*

Why now? Why would the Israeli government signal open-
ness to Syria in the wake of a war with Hezbollah that looked,
at best, like a Pyrrhic victory for Israel, and at worst like a win
for Hezbollah?

The timing of Israel's message could not have been more
propitious. It was, if anything, long overdue. If the ceasefire is
to hold, if Hezbollah's victory is to be transformed into a re-
sounding defeat, if Israel is to snatch political triumph from
the uncertain jaws of combat, there could be no greater boon
to Israeli security than to offer Syria a potent political incentive to dry up Hezbollah's weapons flow from Iran and Syria
itself, to withdraw Syria's backing for Hamas and re-align itself with the West, isolating Iran.

A Strategy That Has Worked

The United States and and Israel adopted just such a strategy
when Egypt was wooed away from the Soviet orbit into a
peace treaty with Israel and an alliance with the United States.

With the promise of U.S. and European economic rewards, and the prospect of regaining the Golan Heights taken by Israel from Syria in the 1967 war, the young Syrian president, Bashar Assad, might achieve for his nation what his father, Hafez, failed to accomplish in a lifetime.

It behooves us to recall that before Egyptian President Anwar Sadat issued his public offer to talk peace with Israel in Jerusalem, Prime Minister [Menachem] Begin sent messages to Sadat through various secret channels via [U.S.] President [Jimmy] Carter and Romanian President Nicolae Ceausescu that Israel was prepared to make major territorial concessions in return for a full peace treaty, and inviting Sadat to meet Begin.

Israeli Foreign Minister Moshe Dayan traveled incognito to Morocco to meet Sadat's deputy prime minister, Hasan Tuhami, who informed Sadat that Israel would agree to a complete withdrawal from the Sinai in exchange for full peace. The secret diplomacy gave Sadat the confidence to issue his public offer to talk peace with Israel, leading to his historic visit and the Egyptian-Israeli peace treaty.

Test the waters now for prying Syria away from Iran, Hezbollah and Hamas, dealing a body blow to radical Islamism.

If such behind-the-scenes messages are not being carried by third parties between Israel and Syria today, they will be tomorrow. These efforts, combined with the Israeli government's public willingness to entertain full withdrawal for full peace with Syria and a resumption of negotiations, are the best way to examine Syria's intentions. If Assad acts to curtail Hezbollah's weapons flow, and his rhetoric softens, we can expect the clandestine dialogue—and the public denials—to intensify, and Assad to take further steps forward, leading eventually to an eruption of overt diplomacy.

Only a rank political and military amateur would fail to thoroughly test the waters now for prying Syria away from Iran, Hezbollah and Hamas, dealing a body blow to radical Islamism. There is no task more urgent. But will the Bush administration abandon reckless fantasies of Syrian regime change—which could bring Islamists to power or chaos—and play ball?

11

The United States Should Negotiate with Iran

Abbas Maleki

Abbas Maleki is currently a senior research fellow at the Belfer Center for Science and International Affairs at Harvard University. He is also an assistant professor at Sharif University of Technology in Tehran, Iran.

Just as the United States is a superpower of the Western world, Iran is a significant power in the Middle East whose influence should be used to greater extent to solve regional and global problems. Iran is ready and willing to collaborate with other countries, including the United States, in defeating terrorist organizations such as al Qaeda. Even among those organizations it does not necessarily see as terrorist groups, such as Hezbollah, it has considerable influence that could be used toward moderating these groups' activities. Iran is also willing to negotiate with the West concerning its nuclear capabilities. Lastly, Iran's oil and gas resources have great potential for easing global energy prices. If the United States and the rest of the world were willing to talk with Iran, there would be much to gain for both sides.

The world faces different crises all the time, and each generation feels its crises to be the biggest. But nobody can ignore the fact that recent developments in certain parts of the world are having a major impact on the relations between nations and peoples.

The [July 2006] North Korean missile tests, the terrorist attack on trains in India, the nuclear standoff with Iran, mas-

Abbas Maleki, "Why Not Involve Iran in Effort to Establish Order in Mideast?" *Forward*, July 21, 2006, pp. 1–2. Reproduced by permission of the author.

sive sectarian turmoil in Iraq, oil prices at unprecedented levels, the capture of Israeli soldiers by Hezbollah and Israeli raids into Lebanon that have resulted in the deaths of more than 200 civilians—these are just a few examples of the crises humanity is facing today.

There are two ways to deal with these developments. One is to impose unilateral solutions that concentrate on only a small part of the world community, and that benefit only a slice of the world's population, such as Western countries. The other way is to approach these problems from a holistic point of view, with the participation of different actors, and with the aim of benefiting a greater number of nations, including those in Asia and the Middle East.

Iran's Regional Significance

It seems that most of the crises in the Eastern Hemisphere, and the propositions for solving them at the state level, involve two common players: the United States and Iran. There have been plenty of analyses of America's position as the only superpower, but less on Iran's role as a regional power in the Middle East, the Persian Gulf, the Caspian region, and Central and Western Asia.

If you look at the performance of Iran's Islamic Republic, it is clear despite all of the difficulties it has faced—the problems, the turmoil and the wars all around Iran—the system has survived. This is not accidental; rather it shows that the Iranian system has checks and balances—think tanks and consultative bodies as well as other structures and processes for rational decision-making—that permit the system to achieve optimum results.

If it is true that Iran is a major player in the turbulent areas of the Middle East and in the energy market, then why can we not use the influence of such a country to help establish regional order and solve global crises?

The major global crises the world is facing can be divided into three categories: terrorism, nuclear and energy.

Iran has a good reputation in the Islamic world, and so Iran can be influential in the war against terrorism.

Collaborating against Terrorism

When it comes to terrorism, the problem is mainly rooted in extremism. Extremism exists not only in the Muslim world, but also in Christianity, Judaism and Hinduism. The demise of terrorism inside Muslim communities is not possible without the participation of religious leaders and statesmen. As a country with a stable government, which includes the participation of respected Muslim clerics, Iran has a good reputation in the Islamic world, and so Iran can be influential in the war against terrorism.

Insurgencies can be classified into two categories. The first is those groups that Iran and the United States agree to be terrorist organizations. These include Al Qaeda, the Taliban, Hizb-ul Tahrir in Central Asia, Sepah Sahabeh in Pakistan, and the Mujahedeen-e Khalq. The elimination of terrorism by these groups suits Iran, and so Iran is ready to cooperate in the areas of media relations, social affairs, intelligence and perhaps even military strikes. Iran has vast amounts of intelligence and information on these groups, having monitored their activities and their predecessors's going as far back as several decades.

A Moderating Influence

The second form of insurgencies includes those groups about which the United States and Iran can have a legitimate disagreement over their characterization as terrorist organizations. These include Hezbollah, Hamas and Islamic Jihad.

However, even with this category Iran could be a key to moderating their activities, because Iran has some influence over these groups. For example, while I personally believe the [July 2006] exacerbation of the conflict in Lebanon was the consequence of overreaction by Israel—specifically the aggressive display by Israeli warplanes over President Bashar Assad's summer palace in Latakia—there is no doubt that Iran wields a great deal of influence over Hezbollah.

Ultimately, the conflict with Lebanon cannot be resolved without some form of political compromise, and Iran has showed in the past that it can play a constructive role in calming the region—as it did in 1993 and again in 1996, in the negotiation of a cease-fire agreement and exchange of prisoners between Lebanon and Israel. In Palestine, Iran can also play a constructive role and help reach a compromise, since other players in that conflict recognize the Islamic Republic as an influential force for stability in the region, while persistent attacks by Israel on the Occupied Territories have in the past merely deteriorated the situation.

Iran has the second-largest proven oil and gas reserves in the world.

Nuclear and Energy Capabilities

Regarding the nuclear issue, Iran is seeking a face-saving resolution that maintains a minimum degree of access to nuclear technology inside Iran. The incentives proposed to Iran by the "5+1 group"—the five permanent members of the United Nations Security Council, plus Germany—are exactly the sort of things that Iran's economy and industries need. Iran simply wants to see better-defined and better-clarified terms in the incentive offer, something that is not very hard for the other side to provide. Addressing Iran's nuclear concerns can only strengthen the Non-Proliferation Treaty [an international treaty, signed by 189 nations including Iran, intended to stop the spread of nuclear weapons] and ease the way for new steps to be taken together in the global effort against the threats posed by nuclear weapons and nuclear stockpiles.

Finally, regarding the energy issue it should be noted Iran has the second-largest proven oil and gas reserves in the world. There are still vast regions in Iran with oil potential that have not been studied in the past because of political conditions or technology limitations.

Iran's energy capabilities on oil, gas, pipelines, electrical power plants and its access to neighboring countries are unique. Iran has common oil and gas fields with 10 of its neighbors and can exchange electricity with all 15 neighbors. Working in Iran's oil and gas fields means better accessibility to Iraqi, Persian Gulf and Caspian Basin fields. Any easing of America's hard sanctions against investment on Iran's oil sector will tend to improve the crisis situation in world energy prices. International oil companies are ready to engage in business and energy cooperation between Iran and the United States, which will have a positive impact on both the world economy and energy security.

Every war ultimately ends with talks. Regional stability serves the interests of Iran, the United States and the rest of the world. Iran is a key player in its region, and can employ its legitimate influence toward calming the situation. Iran and the United States have many interests in common, and the two nations can ultimately overcome their differences by emphasizing their common interests.

12

The United States Should Not Negotiate with Iran

Kathryn Jean Lopez

A conservative editorialist, journalist, and speaker, Kathryn Jean Lopez is the editor of National Review Online *and an associate editor for* National Review. *She has also worked at the Heritage Foundation, a conservative Washington, D.C., think tank.*

The United States has claimed that it opposes tyranny and supports democratic reformers around the world but by offering to negotiate with the repressive regime in Iran, the United States undermines these reformers. The United States ought to be reaching out to aid the reformers, not negotiate with Tehran, as history shows such reformers can be a force for revolutionary change.

On May 31 [2006], Secretary of State Condoleezza Rice announced that the United States would negotiate with Iran if they agreed to stop uranium enrichment. If Iran did not agree to the sit-down on those conditions, there would be sanctions from the likes of Europe, Russia (who adamantly have not been fans of sanctions against Iran)—and the United Nations. President Bush seemed hopeful, confident that "this problem can be solved diplomatically."

We really have no business negotiating with the leader of a nation who considers us an enemy and wants one of our

Kathryn Jean Lopez, "How Does That Translate in Persian? Sending Mixed Signals to the Iranians," *National Review Online*, June 14, 2006. Kathryn Jean Lopez © 2008, dist. by Newspaper Enterprise Association. Reproduced by permission of United Media Enterprises. www.nationalreview.com/.

dearest allies in the Middle East [Israel] wiped off the map. However, reasonable people must debate these proposed diplomatic tactics. There really are no easy answers when it comes to Iran. But one cannot help but wonder: How was Rice's announcement received by the oppressed of Iran?

Most likely as confusion.

Undermining Democracy Activists

As our new Iranian policy was announced (immediately available in Persian translation on the State Department's website) the human-rights group Reporters Without Borders released an alert that it was "very worried" about the well-being of one particular student blogger in Tehran [the Iranian capital]. Abed Tavancheh had been unreachable by his family and friends after pro-democracy demonstrations on his campus. On his blog, translated as "in the name of man, justice, and truth," Tavancheh often posts photos from these daring protests. The last post before Reporters Without Borders announced their concern included the text of a letter by an imprisoned lawyer who unwisely spoke out on behalf of families of journalists and others killed in a 1998 crackdown by the Iranian regime.

> With America's policy concerning negotiations with Iran in constant flux, some oppressed future leaders must wonder what exactly friends are for.

For folks like Tavancheh and his family, the offer from Washington had to sound like the rhetorical and moral equivalent of a punch in the gut—and thus a crushing blow to our eyes and ears on the inside. Tavancheh and other democracy activists may be our best hope in Iran and the region, so crucial to fighting the war on terror. Like Lech Walesa and Solidarity in Poland before the fall of the Soviet Union, many experts point to Iranian labor unions and largely pro-Western students—in a country where about 70 percent of the population is under 30—as the soldiers of a democratic revolution. They're the Iranians we want to be negotiating with, lending a hand to.

The Bush administration has had a somewhat consistently confusing policy regarding Iran—in the first term, one senior State Department official inexplicably publicly referred to the oppressive regime as a "democracy"—which it is most definitely not. But with the high-on-freedom talk the president used to ring in his second term, and this administration's occasional messages and commitments to dissidents, there has been reason for Iranian people to believe they had a friend in America. Just last year [in 2005], President Bush proclaimed, "All who live in tyranny and hopelessness can know: the United States will not ignore your oppression, or excuse your oppressors. When you stand for your liberty, we will stand with you. Democratic reformers facing repression, prison, or exile can know: America sees you for who you are: the future leaders of your free country." But with America's policy concerning negotiations with Iran in constant flux, some oppressed future leaders must wonder what exactly friends are for.

Supporting Its Real Friends

It's not just Iranian dissidents who got punched in the gut by Secretary Rice's announcement. In Egypt, blogger Alaa Seif al-Islam sits in jail for criticizing the government there. What does America's agreement to negotiate with a regime that clearly does not stand with us say to voices for freedom like him? Our words and policies can have a chilling effect on world events—and on the hearts of true freedom fighters, the type of person who is willing to put his life at risk to blog or otherwise tell some truth about the regime he suffers under, giving support to his fellow dissidents, and clueing the rest of us in.

In the days after his second inaugural address, even conservative supporters of President Bush criticized him for being a bit too pie-eyed in his freedom talk. The least we could be doing, however, is lending more support, rhetorical and otherwise to our real friends. The continued mixed signals, however, that negotiation offers to a regime of terror masters, is not the way to contribute to any freedom project.

13

The United States Should Negotiate with Sunni Insurgents in Iraq

Joe Conason

Joe Conason is a national correspondent for the National Observer, *a columnist for* Salon, *and the author of several books, including the best seller* Big Lies: The Right-Wing Propaganda Machine and How It Distorts the Truth.

President George W. Bush continues to argue that a withdrawal of troops from Iraq would leave that country's citizens in the hands of foreign terrorist organizations like al Qaeda and ruin American credibility. These allegations are untrue, as is the insistence that there is only one course of action the United States can take in Iraq. The option that few politicians will acknowledge is for the U.S.-led coalition and the Iraqi government to start negotiations with the Sunni insurgency. In fact, U.S. officers have already begun such discussions, though the American media has underreported it. In other news sources, Sunni politicians report that progress is being made toward an eventual cease-fire. Insurgents have told reporters that when the United States announces a withdrawal date, they will stop fighting and expel al Qaeda from Iraq. Clearly, the best strategy for both Iraq and the coalition forces is to engage in serious negotiations with the Sunni insurgents.

Joe Conason, "Only One Option?" *Salon*, February 3, 2006. This article first appeared in Salon.com, at http://www.Salon.com. An online version remains in the *Salon* archives. Reprinted with permission.

In [his 2006] State of the Union address, George W. Bush proved again his preference for the rhetoric of deception. Unable to marshal a convincing argument for his war in Iraq yet determined to silence his critics, Bush insisted that for patriotic Americans there is simply no choice except his failing strategy.

"A sudden withdrawal of our forces from Iraq would abandon our Iraqi allies to death and prison, would put men like [Osama] bin Laden and [Abu Musab al-] Zarqawi in charge of a strategic country, and show that a pledge from America means little," he warned. "However we feel about the decisions and debates of the past our nation has only one option: We must keep our word, defeat our enemies, and stand behind the American military in this vital mission."

Predictably those clichés won strong applause—who doesn't clap when the president demands support for U.S. troops?—but as usual the bid for inspiration concealed more than a bit of deception.

Would the withdrawal of our forces leave Baghdad to al-Qaida? No, because the foreign-led jihadists represent a small fraction of the insurgency. Must we continue the occupation indefinitely to prove that we "stand behind" the American military? No, because the war is damaging our military strength, and to support the troops means finding a way out of the sand trap as swiftly as possible. And is there "only one option" for the American nation? That's wrong too, although the Democratic leadership didn't dare say so in the feeble response delivered by Virginia Gov. Tim Kaine.

"There's a better way," Kaine repeated like a mantra, but he never bothered to tell us what that might be. The answer is straightforward, is honorable and might even succeed: The United States, its coalition partners and the Iraqi government must open serious negotiations with the Sunni insurgency, aiming toward a durable cease-fire and a timetable for American withdrawal. There need be no political penalty for advocating such negotiations because U.S. officers have already pursued discussions with Iraqi insurgents—and because those discussions represent official policy in Iraq.

Success of Talks So Far

The U.S. media has devoted little space to those talks, but the *Washington Post* and the British press have occasionally reported on them. [In 2005], the *Sunday Times* of London revealed that American officers had participated in two meetings with insurgent leaders in a villa north of Baghdad. Among those in attendance were representatives of the Ansar al-Sunna army, the group responsible for the atrocious mess hall bombing at the U.S. base near Mosul, Iraq, in December 2004. Secretary of Defense Donald Rumsfeld and Gen. John Abizaid both confirmed that those talks had taken place—and that many more meetings had occurred in hopes of "splitting" the insurgency.

> *According to [Sunni leader al-Dulaimi], the weekly meetings between his party and the insurgents have encouraged hope for an eventual cease-fire.*

[In early February 2006], news of peace talks with the insurgents surfaced again. The United Nations news service, IRIN, reported that Sunni politicians claimed to be making progress in discussions with insurgent leaders, while confronting an obstacle that remains beyond their control. "For the last month we've been trying to convince militias to put down their guns until they see whether or not the new government can bring positive results," said Adnan al-Dulaimi, one of the leaders of the Iraqi Accord Front, a Sunni Islamist coalition that supports participation in the political process. According to him, the weekly meetings between his party and the insurgents have encouraged hope for an eventual cease-fire.

"We've made good progress," he said. "But the presence of foreign troops could cause this accord to fail at any time." That is hardly surprising, since recent polls indicate that about 80 percent of Iraqis want Washington and Baghdad to set a date for when the occupation will end.

The IRIN article quoted a man known as Abu Omar, identified as a leader of the insurgent Muhammad army in Anbar province. He confirmed that his group and several others had approved a possible cease-fire, but vowed: "We will quit fighting only if the U.S. military gives us a date for its withdrawal."

The End of al-Qaida in Iraq?

Then the insurgent leader hinted that serious negotiations could not only extricate our troops from Iraq but simultaneously create the conditions for an important victory against our real enemy.

"We're more open to the possibility of improvements in Iraq," said the insurgent commander, "but al-Qaeda doesn't care for such things because it's not composed of Iraqis. It's made up of foreigners who have come to exploit the differences between our brothers."

> *The negotiations that have occurred already . . . show another way home for our troops.*

The meaning of Omar's remarks could hardly be clearer. He and his insurgent comrades will end their murderous rebellion against the Iraqi government if and when they can be assured that U.S. troops will withdraw. And when they are assured that we will leave, they will turn on al-Qaida and either wipe it out or expel it from Iraq.

If the Bush administration insists that we must "defeat" the insurgency, or stand up an Iraqi army that can pacify the country, then negotiations are useless. If Bush insists on identifying all of the insurgents with al-Qaida, then there isn't anyone with whom we can negotiate. If the American objective is to create large permanent bases and to win control of Iraqi oil, then our troops cannot leave and the bloody conflict will grind on without any foreseeable conclusion.

The negotiations that have occurred already, fitful though they may be, show another way home for our troops. The president's claim that we have "only one option" in Iraq is untrue—and the alternative is far more likely to advance the interests of America and the civilized world.

Too bad we have no politician with the wisdom and stature to say so.

14

Private Negotiations with Terrorists Are Increasing

Rod Nordland

Rod Nordland is chief foreign correspondent for Newsweek *and is based in London. He reported from* Newsweek's *Baghdad bureau from 2003 to 2005.*

In Amman, Jordan, Hisham Taleb Ezza's extended family is trying to raise the five hundred thousand dollars his Iraqi kidnappers are demanding for his ransom. This scenario has become common in Iraq, where kidnapping is a rapidly growing business. After successfully extorting large sums of money from foreigners, like the one paid for Italians Simona Pari and Simona Torretta, the ransoms are going up in price. Most coalition countries have signed a pact, pledging not to pay ransoms to terrorists. Still, few of these countries do much to stop private negotiations. The more these negotiations are allowed to continue, the more the terrorists will demand.

The phone rang at 7:05 p.m. in Amman. Muhammed Ezza nearly knocked over a table as he grabbed the receiver. It was five minutes past the deadline that had been set by his brother's Iraqi abductors for a reply to their $500,000 ransom demand. Three dozen of Hisham Taleb Ezza's kinsmen— brothers, cousins and in-laws—waited together in a room in the Jordanian capital. They had no way to scrape up such a fortune, but they were ready to empty their bank accounts, borrow against their pensions and sell their cars for anything they could raise. Hisham had been working in Baghdad as an accountant for Starlight, a transport company with U.S. military contracts in Iraq, when gunmen seized him on Oct. 2 [2004]. Starlight's general director, a Jordanian named Muhammed Ajlouni, had quickly agreed to shut down the company's Iraqi operations, as the kidnappers ordered, but he said he couldn't raise a half-million dollars. "If you can't get the money," the kidnappers told the Ezzas, "kill Ajlouni instead." The family was given 72 hours to think it over.

But [the] 7:05 call was not from the kidnappers. It was only Hisham's wife, frantic for news of her husband. "She's sitting there with two of their daughters on her lap, crying," Muhammed told the men sitting around him. There was nothing they could do but wait for the phone to ring again—and pray.

Italian authorities not only bargained with the kidnappers but apparently delivered a $1 million ransom.

A score of families around the world were holding similarly desperate vigils [that] week. Their loved ones had fallen victim to one of Iraq's fastest-growing enterprises: kidnapping. Abduction as a terror tactic still gets the main share of international attention, as in the case of the British captive Kenneth Bigley. He was one of at least seven hostages beheaded by terrorists in Iraq [in one week in October 2004], and his murder was videotaped by Tawhid and Jihad, an organization led by the notorious Abu Mussab al-Zarqawi. So far, no fewer than 17 different groups have claimed responsibility for kidnapping foreigners in Iraq. Of roughly 150 foreign hostages altogether, about 40 have been killed and at least 20 are still being held. "Iraq is the Olympic stadium where the jihadists get to show off their specialties," says Giandomenico Pico, a former U.N. hostage negotiator.

Rising Hostage Prices

The problem is compounded by the wildfire spread of abduction for profit. Ransom kidnappings have plagued the people of Iraq ever since the [2003 U.S.] invasion. But [from July to October 2004] or so, criminal groups, inspired by the terrorists' kidnapping spree, have discovered that the going rate of $5,000 or $10,000 for an Iraqi hostage is nothing beside the money they can extort from foreigners. Italians welcomed the release of Simona Pari and Simona Torretta, the Italian aid workers who were dragged in broad daylight from their offices in downtown Baghdad on Sept. 7 [2004]. But the joy has been soured by public confirmation that Italian authorities not only bargained with the kidnappers but apparently delivered a $1 million ransom. Now hostage prices are soaring. [In September 2004] a prosperous Jordanian businessman in Iraq haggled his kidnappers down to $80,000 from $1 million. Now Ezza's kidnappers are asking half a million for a bookkeeper.

Most of the 30-odd Coalition countries publicly supported a U.S.-sponsored pact, pledging not to pay ransom to terrorists. Still, few of the member states do anything to stop private negotiations. The Turkish government gave its blessing when a Turkish truckers' association caved in to hostage-takers and pulled its drivers out of Iraq. "The life of our citizens is more important," said a Turkish official who is working to free hostages. After Ezza's captors demanded $500,000, his family asked the Jordanian chargé d'affaires in Baghdad what to do. "He said just try to negotiate a price you can pay," says Muhammed Ezza. A Jordanian official in Amman says his government's policy is not to negotiate with terrorists—but not to prevent the families of hostages from cutting their own deals. At least a dozen Jordanians have been freed that way. And Amman's definition of "negotiate with terrorists" is flexible. "We have our relationships with the Iraqi tribes in the

Sunni Triangle," the official says. "We are playing politics, doing backstage deals with the tribes, doing our best to save [hostages]."

Doing Business with Terrorists

The Italian government denies paying $1 million for the Simonas, but doesn't deny that such a ransom was paid. "More than 16 negotiations took place to free the Simonas," says intelligence chief Nicolo Pollari. One Kuwaiti newspaper, *Al Rai al Aam*, evidently had a source inside the kidnappers' group, the self-styled Islamic Army of Iraq. The paper's editor in chief, Jassim Booday, says the group got half the money when go-betweens were allowed to see the hostages. The other $500,000 was delivered on their release. "In principle we shouldn't give in to blackmail, but this time we had to," says Gustavo Selva, head of the Foreign Affairs Committee in Italy's Parliament. "Although it's a dangerous path."

Ransom kidnappers want to do business.

But a tempting one. Ransom kidnappers want to do business. There's little point in trying to negotiate with jihadists like al-Zarqawi, whose dream is an all-out war between Muslims and the West. Bigley's abductors kept him alive for weeks while he begged for his life. His family denounced the war. Dublin declared him to be an Irish citizen, based on his grandmother's nationality, in hopes that his captors would see him as a struggling, anti-imperialist underdog. Libyan leader Muammar Kaddafi, no great friend of the West himself, made a personal plea for the British hostage's life. Nothing helped. "It's Bigley's bad luck that he was captured by the most ruthless of the groups," says Booday. (The BBC reported that he was killed after a failed escape attempt.)

Desperate Families

The Ezzas still have hope, but not much else. Muhammed blames Hisnam's boss for not putting up the ransom. He says he warned Ajlouni: "The blood of my brother will be on your hands." Ajlouni complained to Jordanian authorities that the Ezzas were threatening to take revenge on him if Hisham dies. "I'm trying to do everything I can to free him," he tells *Newsweek*. "I've already put 76 people out of work by shutting down in Iraq. But I just don't have half a million dollars." He says he thinks the kidnappers are former employees with a personal grudge against him. "I told the family I will take on this matter until the end."

The cousins debated the point . . . waiting for the phone to ring. "He sent 5,000 trucks to Iraq, of course he can pay," said one. "He wants to help, but they have to negotiate." "No, he's a son of a bitch." The phone rang, and everyone fell silent. Another false alarm.

The sun was rising Thursday morning when the phone rang again. A glance at the screen showed Hisham's number. The kidnappers have been using his mobile phone to contact the family.

Hisham was on the line: "Muhammed, how are you? How is the family?"

"Good, thank God."

"You need to be strong to take care of my kids."

"Inshallah, you'll come back to your kids."

"Try to get that money, even though I know it's not within your means. Here, talk to the man here." A kidnapper came on the line.

"If I sell everything under me and over me, I can only get $15,500," said Muhammed.

"It's not enough. You're a big family. Force Ajlouni to pay."

"The financial situation is difficult. We can't do it, we're being watched."

"Cut it short. You have two days. $500,000, or give us Ajlouni." The kidnapper hung up. Muhammed slumped into the nearest chair, tears streaming down his cheeks.

15

The United States Should Negotiate with al Qaeda

Louise Richardson

Louise Richardson is executive dean of the Radcliffe Institute for Advanced Study and a lecturer on terrorism and international security at Harvard University and Harvard Law School.

In the war on terrorism, the United States has operated under the assumption that its enemies' demands are unreasonable and nonnegotiable. But it would be wise to find out if this assumption is, indeed, correct. America currently has an opportunity to negotiate with al Qaeda, and it should take advantage of it. This will no doubt be an unpopular suggestion; yet, historically, many governments have negotiated with terrorist organizations. Negotiations provide an invaluable chance to learn about one's adversaries. America's ignorance of al Qaeda up to this point has had substantial negative consequences. If the U.S. government were to hold talks with al Qaeda, it would learn whether their demands are reasonable and if they are not, where their vulnerabilities are and how best to exploit them.

If anything, [Americans] appear to know less about the nature of our adversaries in the war on terrorism than we did when we began. We take as a given that their demands are so extreme as to be nonnegotiable, but it would be worth finding out if that is, in fact, the case. Yet suggestions that their demands might be negotiable are treated with deep suspicion,

From *What Terrorists Want: Understanding the Terrorist Threat*, by Louise Richardson. Copyright © 2006 by Louise Richardson. Used by permission of Random House, Inc., and John Murray (Pulishers) Limited.

and suggestions that we actually talk to the terrorists are considered tantamount to treason. It seems to me that this issue is of such importance that it needs to be demonstrated rather than simply asserted that their demands indeed are nonnegotiable. Even if we could get over the public's inhibition against talking to the terrorists it would not be altogether easy to do so. The hammer of American military power that descended on al-Qaeda in the fall of 2001 had the effect of shattering the organization and sending splinters throughout the world, so it is not entirely clear to whom one could talk. That said, Ayman al-Zawahiri has clearly emerged as the chief spokesman and strategist of the al-Qaeda leadership, and while it is far from clear that he has the authority to carry his followers with him, the opportunity to engage him is one that should not be missed, no matter how much opprobrium we hold for him.

I have no illusions about how unpopular a suggestion this is likely to be. Governments always resist talking to terrorists for fear that it will seem to confer legitimacy on them, or to reward their terrorism. It is also the case that many governments have successfully defeated terrorist groups without ever engaging them. Nevertheless, it is also the case that Britain ended the IRA's [Irish Republican Army] terrorism only through negotiating with the terrorists and that the cease-fire currently enjoyed in Sri Lanka is a result of government talks with the hated Tamil Tigers. The difference between the [Italian terrorist group the] Red Brigades and [Germany's] RAF [Red Army Faction], on the one hand, and the LTTE [Liberation Tigers of Tamil Eelam] and IRA, on the other, is that the first pair both had nonnegotiable goals and were isolated from their communities. The second pair had political and hence negotiable goals and a significant degree of support in their communities. . . . The two key characteristics of all terrorist groups are the nature of the goals they seek and the nature of their relationship to their community. Al-Qaeda appears to have nonnegotiable goals and a significant degree of community support. The focus of our intelligence, and indeed all other counterterrorist policies at the moment, ought to be, first, to establish if that indeed is the nature of their goal and, second, to isolate them from their community of support.

Ending Conflicts Sooner

Wars are easier to begin than to end; they tend to last much longer than an objective assessment of the interests of the participants suggest that they should. The same is true of terrorism and counterterrorist campaigns. In some cases one side has overwhelming power and simply wins the conflict, but this is rarely the case. The First World War, for example, ended in 1918 on terms that had essentially been available two years earlier. The Boer War could have ended on the same terms as it eventually did eighteen months earlier [than it did]. The IRA finally called an end to its campaign seven years after the Good Friday Agreement, and the broad terms of that agreement could have been available many years earlier. There are a variety of reasons for this. The costs of wars are such that participants feel they need to continue fighting to justify the costs already borne. Wars and terrorist campaigns tend to be prolonged by an unlikely alliance of hawks on both sides and generally require an alliance of doves on both sides in order to make peace.

Talks with terrorists are . . . an invaluable opportunity for gaining information about the opponent.

In the case of terrorist groups, delay can be caused by unwillingness to negotiate. Talks with terrorists are not simply an opportunity for negotiating concessions, they are also an invaluable opportunity for gaining information about the opponent. Governments tend to be reluctant to get involved in talks with terrorists as they do not want to confer legitimacy on an illegal group or to reward its violent activity. Nevertheless, many states have, in fact, talked to terrorists, although most have been inconsistent in their willingness to do so. The Khasavyurt Accord brought the first Chechen war to an end with the promise of resolving the status of Chechnya, but the outbreak of the second Chechen war and [Russian Federation president] Vladimir Putin's assumption of power and firm refusal to negotiate have meant a bloody prolongation of the conflict.

There are any number of examples of how our ignorance of our enemies has served only to strengthen them.

Historic Negotiation Successes

Throughout the conflict in Northern Ireland, the British government held talks with the IRA. These talks often took place during a time when the government had an official line of refusing to talk to terrorists. From the first secret talks in 1972, which served mainly to demonstrate to each side the extent of the differences between them, the meetings helped the British government size up its opponent. In 1975, a series of meetings was held between the British government and the IRA while the movement maintained a cease-fire. The IRA subsequently concluded that it had been tricked into the meetings. Initially it was led to believe that Britain was looking for a way to extricate itself from the province, but it concluded that the talks had been a ruse by the government to gather intelligence and encourage splits within the movement by trying to draw some members into constitutional politics. The years of direct and indirect public and private talks finally paid off in the signing of the 1998 Good Friday Agreement.

By overcoming our reluctance to talk, we could discover a great deal about our adversaries, about the importance they assign to particular goals, about how they make decisions, and about their assessment of their own position. Such talks do not have to be public, nor do they have to be direct. They could be conducted through intermediaries, but it is very difficult to know your enemies if you don't try to engage them.

Lack of Knowledge Has Hurt Us

There are any number of examples of how our ignorance of our enemies has served only to strengthen them. In his speech to the United Nations in February 2003, when Colin Powell painted the portrait of Abu Mus'ab al-Zarqawi as bin Laden's man in Iraq, he suddenly transformed al-Zarqawi, a hitherto largely unknown two-bit Jordanian thug, into a leader of a global movement. At the time al-Zarqawi was not remotely in the same league as the highly trained, highly educated, experienced leadership of al-Qaeda. By offering a $25 million reward for him, we soon elevated him into the senior ranks. In fact, it took al-Zarqawi a year and a half to declare allegiance to bin Laden in a statement posted on Islamist Web sites. Two months later, in December 2004, bin Laden, in an audiotape, accepted al-Zarqawi's fealty and pronounced him the "emir" of al-Qaeda in Iraq and instructed Muslims to listen to him.

By knowing your enemies, you can find out what it is they want. Once you know what they want, you can then decide whether to deny it to them and thereby demonstrate the futility of their tactic, give it to them, or negotiate and give them a part of it in order to cause them to end their campaign. By knowing your enemies, you can make an assessment not just of their motives but also of their capabilities and of the caliber of their leaders and their organizations. Any information one could glean from such encounters would be useful. If one concludes definitively that their demands are nonnegotiable, the focus of one's policy must be to isolate them from their communities and go after them with targeted coercive policies. On the other hand, one might learn that their demands are, in fact, negotiable, and this could once again help to direct counterterrorist policy. The most likely outcomes would be to discover that they are not a unitary actor and that some have negotiable demands and others do not. Then the direction of policy should be to exploit these differences and sow dissent among them.

16

The U.S. Should Not Negotiate with al Qaeda

Andrew C. McCarthy

Andrew C. McCarthy is the director of the Center for Law and Counterterrorism at the Foundation for Defense of Democracies. He is a former federal prosecutor and a regular contributor to National Review Online.

Despite the continued destruction and bloodshed brought upon Americans by al Qaeda, some have suggested that we sign a treaty with this terrorist organization. This would not even meet one of the basic requirements of a treaty, to be signed between nation-states. In 2005, when the Senate Judiciary Committee prepared to question Alberto Gonzales—George W. Bush's nominee for Attorney General of the United States—many criticized Gonzales's comments about the Geneva Conventions. Gonzales's remarks, vastly distorted by the media and leftist critics, merely questioned whether the treatment of detainees prescribed by the Geneva Conventions was appropriate for members of an organization as barbaric as al Qaeda. Gonzales's view, that the Geneva Conventions do not apply to al Qaeda, is far from radical, as critics have labeled it; in fact, it is the viewpoint of a large number of Americans.

Since the early 1990s, al Qaeda has, at the very least, killed American soldiers and desecrated their remains in Somalia; urged the murder of all Americans—civilians and military alike—wherever on the globe they may be found; conducted

Andrew C. McCarthy, "Should We Make a Treaty with al Qaeda?" *National Review Online,* January 15, 2005. Reproduced by permission.

simultaneous sneak attacks on the American embassies in Kenya and Tanzania, resulting in the mass murder of over 240 civilians (the vast majority of them Muslims and non-Americans); killed 17 American seamen in an attempt to blow up the destroyer, the U.S.S. *Cole*; murdered 3,000 Americans in hijack attacks on the World Trade Center and the Pentagon; and spearheaded guerrilla wars in Afghanistan and Iraq that have killed well over a thousand American military personnel and countless civilians.

In addition to killing civilians in sneak attacks—commonly, detonating bombs within nondescript cars parked or driven in broad daylight in densely populated areas—they also secrete themselves among their once and future victims. They wear no distinguishing insignia to segregate themselves as a militia. They use mosques and schools and hospitals to plan and store weaponry. They feign surrender and then open fire on unsuspecting coalition forces attempting the civilized act of detaining, rather than shooting, them. As for treatment of their own detainees, their practice ranges from execution-style homicide to beastly beheading—usually captured on film and circulated on the Internet to buck up the other savages while scaring the living hell out of everyone else.

So here's an idea: Let's make a treaty with them.

Let's reward this behavior with a grant of honorable-combatant status. Let's give them the same kind of benefits the Geneva Conventions reserve for soldiers who play by the rules: who identify themselves as soldiers; who don't intentionally murder civilians; who do not threaten schools, hospitals, and houses of worship by turning them into military targets; who grant quarter honorably; and who treat their captives with dignity and respect. Let's provide al Qaeda with "amenities such as dormitories, kitchenettes, sports equipment, canteens, and a monthly pay allowance in Swiss francs"—the Geneva prescriptions for POWs [Prisoners of War] that Lee A.

Casey and David Rivkin Jr. outline with characteristic clarity in the current issue of *National Review*.

Not a Nation-State

Of course, we'll have to find someone from al Qaeda able to sign the treaty. This is no small issue. Leaving aside the whole fugitive-on-the-lam problem, treaties, you see, are signed between and among *nation states*. Many nation states are repressive, but the nation-state as a concept is generally thought to be a human good—an organizing arrangement under which a variegated society can flourish. Al Qaeda, of course, is not a nation state. It is an international terrorist network. It's also not too variegated. It exists to terrorize and kill, which tends to chill a vibrant social order.

> *Gonzales has been numbingly libeled for having called the Geneva Conventions "quaint." Naturally, this is not close to what he said.*

Nevertheless, we can surely find someone to ink the deal. News recently broke that Abu Musab Zarqawi just got a big promotion, becoming al Qaeda's "Emir of the Jihad" in Iraq. Sure, it's not exactly our usual conception of a chief executive, a secretary of state, or a foreign minister. But Zarqawi, a Jordanian, finds himself in Iraq because right now that is the best place to kill Americans. That's the skill at which he is sufficiently adept to have gotten the gig because that's exactly what a high official in al Qaeda is supposed to do. Not your idea of the kind of entity you envision the good ol' U.S.A. signing treaties with? You are so 20th century!

In fact, saying such things aloud may make progressive-minded humanitarian activists start thinking of you as one of those troglodytes who actually thinks sitting down to negotiate *anything* with such an entity, or granting it the tiniest concession, legitimizes and empowers it. These, obviously, are the same backward thinkers who have the temerity to suggest that giving Geneva Convention protections to terrorists rewards, therefore encourages, and therefore guarantees more terrorism. Talk about quaint.

The Attack on Gonzales

Quaint, of course, brings us to Alberto Gonzales, the White House counsel nominated by President Bush to be the next attorney general of the United States. Gonzales has been numbingly libeled for having called the Geneva Conventions "quaint." Naturally, this is not close to what he said. Rather, he asserted that the terrorist style of warfare had rendered "quaint" the notion that al Qaeda captives merited such Geneva-based provisions as "commissary privileges, scrip (i.e., advances of monthly pay), athletic uniforms and scientific instruments." Incidentally, he made this statement in a memorandum to his boss—that is, from the White House counsel to the president. In the height of mid-90s scandal, Democrats and the mainstream media tended to view the very thought of intruding on that relationship as an unspeakable violation of the attorney-client privilege and the end of the Bill of Rights as we know it. Now...they want the rest of the memos. Evidently, they've evolved.

This, no doubt, is because Gonzales, aside from being an intimate of the sitting Republican president, is also, alas, one of those sticks-in-the-mud who thinks we shouldn't treat al Qaeda terrorists as if we had a treaty with them, and that we shouldn't accord the privileges and immunities of honorable warfare to barbarians. For such positions has he been castigated by a hastily assembled group of retired military brass with a recent history of anti-Bush activism, the American Civil Liberties Union, and the usual cabal of "human-rights activists" who, though they've never met a terrorist they wouldn't coddle, don't seem to get particularly whipped up over humans whose work day is interrupted by hijacked jumbo jets crashing through office windows.

A Question for Senators

In any event, on Thursday [January 6, 2005], the Senate Judiciary Committee will hold a confirmation hearing for Gonzales. Critics are urging committee Democrats to question the nominee aggressively on the benighted administration policy of no Geneva protections for terrorists whose lives are singularly dedicated to annihilating Americans. Fair game, one supposes, but no senator should be allowed to take up the torch without at least answering a simple question: Do you favor a treaty with al Qaeda?

The inarguable, inconvenient fact is we have no such treaty. Al Qaeda is not and, indeed, cannot be among Geneva's high contracting parties. It is not a country. The U.S. has for over two decades expressly rejected a treaty—the 1977 Protocol I to the Geneva Conventions—that would have vested terrorists with Geneva protections. I hate to spoil the party, but if we're going to have such a treaty with al Qaeda and other terrorist organizations, it will have to be a new one.

> The next attorney general's position on this matter is not a radical view. It's America's view.

Under Article III of the Constitution, the consent of two thirds of the Senate's membership is required before a treaty can be approved. Although we haven't yet been able to arrange getting President Bush and Emir Zarqawi together for a signing ceremony, getting the senators on record—especially given the caviling over Gonzales—could really get the ball rolling. So let's ask them. All of them. Plain and simple, so the folks back home know just where you stand: Do you favor a treaty with al Qaeda?

Does anyone think there are 67 yea votes on that one? How about ten? How about one? No. The fact is, outside a lunatic fringe, there's not a politician in America who would support something so absurd.

The next attorney general's position on this matter is not a radical view. It's America's view. So ask away—it'll be good for all of us to know where everyone stands.

Organizations to Contact

The editors have compiled the following list of organizations concerned with the issues debated in this book. The descriptions are derived from materials provided by the organizations. All have publications or information available for interested readers. The list was compiled on the date of publication of the present volume; the information provided here may change. Be aware that many organizations may take several weeks or longer to respond to inquiries, so allow as much time as possible.

American Enterprise Institute for Public Policy Research (AEI)
1150 Seventeenth St. NW, Washington, DC   20036
(202) 862-5800 • fax: (202) 862-7177
Web site: www.aei.org

The American Enterprise Institute for Public Policy Research is a private, nonpartisan research and education institution dedicated to defending American principles of democratic capitalism, such as limited government, individual liberty, and vigilant and effective defense and foreign policies. It sponsors research classified in three primary divisions: Economic Policy Studies, Social and Political Studies, and Defense and Foreign Policy Studies. Its publications include a monthly newsletter, the *American* magazine, the *Monthly National Security Outlook*, and numerous others.

The American Foreign Policy Council (AFPC)
509 C St. NE, Washington, DC   20002
(202) 543-1006 • fax: (202) 543-1007
Web site: www.afpc.org

The American Foreign Policy Council is a nonprofit organization that provides information and analysis to those who make or influence American foreign policy. AFPC also assists world leaders, particularly in the former USSR, in building democracies. It publishes regular bulletins such as *Foreign Policy Alert, Asia Security Monitor,* and *Eurasia Security Watch.*

The American Israel Public Affairs Committee (AIPAC)
(202) 639-5200
www.aipac.org

The American Israel Public Affairs Committee is a pro-Israel lobbying group. It works with both Democratic and Republican leaders to promote policies that strengthen the U.S.-Israel relationship and promote Israel's security. AIPAC publishes *Near East Report, Middle East Spotlight, Israel Connection, Defense Digest,* and other publications.

The Brookings Institution
1775 Massachusetts Ave. NW, Washington, DC   20036
(202) 797-6000
Web site: www.brookings.edu

The Brookings Institution is a public policy organization that emphasizes strengthening American democracy; supporting the economic and social welfare, security, and opportunity of all Americans; and securing a more open, safe, prosperous, and cooperative international system. It conducts independent research and provides recommendations based on this research that support its three main goals. The institution publishes various newsletters, including *Global Update, Middle East Memo,* and *Center for Northeast Asian Policy Studies Bulletin,* among other publications.

The Carter Center
One Copenhill, 453 Freedom Parkway, Atlanta, GA   30307
(404) 420-5100
e-mail: carterweb@emory.edu
Web site: www.cartercenter.org

The Carter Center works in partnership with Emory University and other organizations toward its goals of ensuring human rights and alleviating human suffering. It specifically works to prevent and resolve conflicts, enhance freedom and democracy, and improve health through research, analysis, and action. The center publishes the newsletter the *Carter Center News* and reports such as "The Israeli-Palestinian Conflict: Historical and Prospective Intervention Analyses."

Cato Institute
1000 Massachusetts Ave. NW, Washington, DC   20001
(202) 842-0200 • fax: (202) 842-3490
Web site: www.cato.org

The Cato Institute is a public policy research foundation that promotes the traditional American principles of limited government, individual liberty, free markets and peace. In addition to research, it provides educational information and encourages greater involvement of citizens in public policy discussions. The institute publishes the daily e-mail newsletter *Daily Dispatch, Cato Journal, Cato Policy Report*, foreign policy briefings, and other publications.

Center for Strategic & International Studies (CSIS)
1800 K St. NW, Washington, DC   20006
(202) 887-0200 • fax: (202) 775-3199
Web site: www.csis.org

The Center for Strategic and International Studies is a bipartisan nonprofit organization seeking to advance global security and prosperity. It serves as a planning partner for government officials in its research, analysis, and policy initiatives. CSIS publishes numerous reports such as "The Evolving Security Situation in Iraq: The Continuing Need for Strategic Patience," "Currents and Crosscurrents of Radical Islam," and the "Transnational Threats Update."

Council on Foreign Relations (CFR)
The Harold Pratt House, 58 E. Sixty-eighth St.
New York, NY   10065
(212) 434-9400 • fax: (212) 434-9800
Web site: www.cfr.org

The Council on Foreign Relations is a nonpartisan think tank that acts as a resource to help government officials, citizens, students, educators, and others better understand the world and the foreign policy decisions facing the United States. It provides current information and analyses of world events and American foreign policy and supports a studies program that promotes independent research. The council does not take institutional positions on policy matters. It publishes the journal *Foreign Affairs*, the newsletters *Daily Brief* and *The World This Week*, Task Force Reports, and numerous other publications.

Foundation for Middle East Peace (FMEP)
1761 N St. NW, Washington, DC   20036
(202) 835-3650 • fax: (202) 835-3651
email: info@fmep.org
Web site: www.fmep.org

The Foundation for Middle East Peace is a nonprofit organization that promotes peace between Israel and Palestine. FMEP offers speakers, sponsors programs, and makes small grants. It publishes the "Report on Israeli Settlement in the Occupied Territories" and other reports, such as "Building Sovereignty in Palestine—a New Paradigm for the Gaza-Egypt Frontier."

The Heritage Foundation
214 Massachusetts Ave. NE, Washington, DC   20002
(202) 546-4400 • fax: (202) 546-8328
Web site: www.heritage.org

The Heritage Foundation is a public policy think tank with emphases on individual liberty, free enterprise, limited government, a strong national defense, and traditional American values. It provides information and research on such issues, and promotes policy. Its publications include the weekly digest *PolicyWire*, and reports such as "Health Care and Homeland Security: Crossroads of Emergency Response."

The Middle East Forum

1500 Walnut St., Ste. 1050, Philadelphia, PA   19102
(215) 546-5406 • fax: (215) 546-5409
e-mail: info@meforum.org
Web site: www.meforum.org

The Middle East Forum is a think tank that promotes American interests—such as fighting radical Islam and working for Palestinian acceptance of Israel—in the Middle East. It actively urges policies that protect Americans and their allies in this region and educates the public about Middle Eastern issues and policy. The forum publishes the *Middle East Quarterly Journal* and special reports such as "Asymmetrical Threat Concept and Its Reflections on International Security."

United Nations (UN)

One United Nations Plaza, New York, NY   10017
Web site: www.un.org

The United Nations is an organization made up of 192 member countries with the goals of international cooperation and collective security, as well as human rights. The UN provides resources to resolve international conflicts and formulate policies that affect its member nations. Among the UN's publications are the quarterlies *UN Chronicle* and *Africa Renewal*, and the twice-monthly *Development Update*.

U.S. Department of Homeland Security

Washington, DC   20528
(202) 282-8000
Web site: www.dhs.gov

The U.S. Department of Homeland Security was established in 2001 to provide a unifying core for the national network of organizations and institutions working to secure the United States. It assesses the nation's vulnerabilities, coordinates with other organizations to ensure the most effective response, and provides information to the American public and state and local governments. The department's publications include Annual Performance Reports, Privacy Impact Assessments, and others.

U.S. Department of State
2201 C St. NW, Washington, DC   20520
(202) 647-4000
Web site: www.state.gov

The U.S. Department of State represents the United States in its relationships with foreign governments, organizations, and individuals. It seeks to promote a more free, prosperous, and secure world. The department publishes *Diplomacy: The U.S. State Department at Work*, as well as *Country Reports on Human Rights Practices, Country Reports on Terrorism* and various other publications.

U.S. Institute of Peace (USIP)
1200 Seventeenth St. NW, Washington, DC   20036
(202) 457-1700 • fax: (202) 429-6063
Web site: www.usip.org

USIP is a nonpartisan organization established and funded by Congress. It is devoted to preventing and resolving violent international conflicts and promoting post-conflict stability. The institute provides conflict management information and resources, and engages in peace-building efforts worldwide. Its publications include the newsletter *PeaceWatch*, Peaceworks reports, and working papers such as "New Hopes for Negotiated Solutions in Colombia."

The Washington Institute for Near East Policy
1828 L St. NW, Ste. 1050, Washington, DC   20036
(202) 452-0650 • fax: (202) 223-5364
Web site: www.washingtoninstitute.org

The Washington Institute for Near East Policy is an organization devoted to the advancement of a balanced and realistic understanding of American interests in the Middle East. Led by a bipartisan board of advisors, the institute promotes an American engagement in the Middle East that is committed to strengthening alliances and friendships and promoting security, peace, prosperity, and democracy for the people in that region. The institute publishes policy papers, *Policy Focus*, military research papers, research notes, and other publications.

Bibliography

Books

William C. Banks, Mitchel B. Wallerstein, and Renée de Nevers — *Combating Terrorism: Strategies and Approaches.* Washington, DC: CQ Press, 2007.

Medea Benjamin and Jodie Evans — *Stop the Next War Now: Effective Responses to Violence and Terrorism.* Novato, CA: New World Library, 2005.

Jane Boulden and Thomas G. Weiss, eds. — *Terrorism and the UN: Before and After September 11.* Bloomington: Indiana University Press, 2004.

Mary Buckley and Rick Fawn, eds. — *Global Responses to Terrorism: 9/11, Afghanistan and Beyond.* New York: Routledge, 2003.

Daniel Byman — *The Five Front War: The Better Way to Fight Global Jihad.* Hoboken, NJ: Wiley, 2008.

Jack Caravelli — *Nuclear Insecurity: Understanding the Threat from Rogue Nations and Terrorists.* Westport, CT: Praeger, 2008.

David Cortright and George A. Lopez, eds. — *Uniting Against Terror: Cooperative Nonmilitary Responses to the Global Terrorist Threat.* Cambridge, MA: MIT Press, 2007.

Chester A. Crocker, Fen Osler Hampson, and Pamela Aall, eds.	*Leashing the Dogs of War: Conflict Management in a Divided World.* Washington, DC: United States Institute of Peace Press, 2007.
Audrey Kurth Cronin and James M. Ludes, eds.	*Attacking Terrorism: Elements of a Grand Strategy.* Washington, DC: Georgetown University Press, 2004.
Marius Deeb	*Syria's Terrorist War on Lebanon and the Peace Process.* New York: Palgrave, 2003.
Alan M. Dershowitz	*Why Terrorism Works: Understanding the Threat, Responding to the Challenge.* New Haven, CT: Yale University Press, 2003.
Adam Dolnik and Keith M. Fitzgerald	*Negotiating Hostage Crises with the New Terrorists.* Westport, CT: Praeger, 2008.
Johan Galtung	*Pax Pacifica: Terrorism, the Pacific Hemisphere, Globalization, and Peace Studies.* Boulder, CO: Paradigm, 2005.
Daniel S. Hamilton, ed.	*Terrorism and International Relations,* Washington, DC: Center for Transatlantic Relations, 2006.
Judith Palmer Harik	*Hezbollah: The Changing Face of Terrorism.* London: Tauris, 2005.
Marianne Heiberg, Brendan O'Leary, and John Tirman, eds.	*Terror, Insurgency, and the State: Ending Protracted Conflicts.* Philadelphia: University of Pennsylvania Press, 2007.

Steve Hewitt

British War on Terror: Terrorism and Counter-terrorism on the Home Front Since 9-11. New York: Continuum International, 2008.

Matthew Levitt

Hamas: Politics, Charity, and Terrorism in the Service of Jihad. New Haven, CT: Yale University Press, 2006.

Giuseppe Nesi, ed.

International Cooperation in Counterterrorism: The United Nations and Regional Organizations in the Fight Against Terrorism. London: Ashgate, 2006.

Paul R. Pillar

Terrorism and U.S. Foreign Policy. Washington, DC: Brookings Institution Press, 2004.

Jerrold M. Post

The Mind of the Terrorist: The Psychology of Terrorism from the IRA to al-Qaeda. New York: Palgrave, 2007.

Bertram I. Spector and I. William Zartman, eds.

Getting It Done: Postagreement Negotiation and International Regimes. Washington, DC: United States Institute of Peace Press, 2003.

Douglas Sturkey

The Limits of American Power: Prosecuting a Middle East Peace. Northampton, MA: Edward Elgar, 2007.

Tamara Cofman Wittes

How Israelis and Palestinians Negotiate: A Cross-Cultural Analysis of the Oslo Peace Process. Washington, DC: United States Institute of Peace Press, 2005.

Periodicals

Yossi Alpher   "Could Israel Make Common Cause
                          with Sunni Arabs?" *Forward*, Febru-
                          ary 9, 2007.

Douglas A. Borer   "Why Not Test Bin Laden's 'Truce'
                          Offer?" *Christian Science Monitor*,
                          January 24, 2006.

David Brooks   "War of Ideology," *New York Times*,
                          July 24, 2004.

Juan Cole   "Israel's Failed-State Strategy," *Salon*,
                          July 7, 2006.

Martin   "Make a Deal with Syria and Weaken
van Creveld   the Iran-Hezbollah Axis," *Forward*,
                          January 26, 2007.

Deborah Fidel   "Annapolis 'Plan,' Like Others, Will
                          Fail," *Jewish Chronicle*, November 15,
                          2007.

Abraham Foxman   "Dialogue with Muslims: Realistic or
                          Pipe Dream?" *Deep South Jewish
                          Voice*, December 2006.

Thomas L.   "Long Spoon Diplomacy," *New York
Friedman   Times*, October 9, 2003.

Newt Gingrich   "Defeat of Terror, Not Roadmap Di-
                          plomacy, Will Bring Peace," *Middle
                          East Quarterly*, Spring 2005.

Martin Griffiths   "Sometimes Talking Is the Lesser
                          Evil," *International Herald Tribune*,
                          June 29, 2006.

Efraim Halevy   "Romancing Iran," *New Republic*, August 14, 2006.

Gary Kamiya   "Last Chance for Mideast Peace," *Salon*, April 3, 2007.

Nicholas D. Kristof   "Wishful Thinking on Korea," *New York Times*, January 10, 2004.

Nick Lane   "Peace Without Negotiations? Not in a Million Years," *Jewish Chronicle*, August 7, 2003.

Michael A. Ledeen   "Talking to Iran," *Wall Street Journal*, August 18, 2007.

Daniel Levy   "Plan B on Israel-Palestine," *American Prospect*, June 22, 2007.

William Maley   "Talking to the Taliban," *World Today*, November 2007.

Suzanne Maloney and Ray Takeyh   "Engage Iran," *Democracy: A Journal of Ideas*, fall 2007.

Hisham Matar   "Seeing What We Want to See in Qaddafi," *New York Times*, February 5, 2007.

Robert Mnookin and Susan Hackley   "Disconnecting 'Quid' from 'Quo,'" *Los Angeles Times*, September 26, 2004.

Peter R. Neumann   "Negotiating with Terrorists," *Foreign Affairs*, January/February 2007.

George Neumayr   "Preemptive Appeasers," *American Spectator*, September 9, 2004.

Danielle Pletka "Diplomacy with the Devil," *New York Times*, November 19, 2007.

Joel Pollak "A Northern Ireland Solution for the West Bank?" *Palestine-Israel Journal of Politics, Economics, and Culture*, vol. 14, no. 2, 2007.

Dana Priest "U.S. Talks with Iraqi Insurgents Confirmed," *Washington Post*, June 27, 2005.

Seymour D. Reich "There Are 'Good' Palestinians to Negotiate With," *New York Jewish Week*, March 23, 2007.

Gidon D. Remba "The Arab Peace Plan: What the Right Doesn't Want You to Know," *Jewish Chronicle*, April 19, 2007.

Gidon D. Remba "Realists Negotiate, Idealists Make War," *Jewish Chronicle*, December 28, 2006.

Gidon D. Remba "What Bush and Olmert Could Learn from Begin and Sadat," *Jewish Chronicle*, December 20, 2007.

J. Philip Rosen "Good Terrorists, Bad Terrorists?" *New York Jewish Week*, March 2, 2007.

Barry Rubin "Negotiations Are Not the Way to Go This Time," *Jewish News Weekly of Northern California*, August 25, 2006.

Barry Rubin "Real Negotiations with Syria? Don't Even Think About It!" *Jewish Exponent*, October 5, 2006.

Afif Safieh   "We Palestinians Will Honor Our
                       Word," *Forward*, February 16, 2007.

Patrick Seale   "How Israel and the U.S. Aim To-
                       ward Disaster," *Arab-American News*,
                       June 23–29, 2007.

Sharif Shuja   "America, North Korea and Iran,"
                       Contemporary Review, Winter 2007.

Fuad Siniora   "Give the Arab Peace Initiative a
                       Chance," *New York Times*, May 11,
                       2007.

Michael Ware   "Talking with the Enemy," *Time*, Feb-
                       ruary 20, 2005.

Robert Wiener   "Rep: We Have to Talk to Hamas,"
                       MetroWest Jewish News, December 6,
                       2007.

Michael Wines   "To Negotiate or Not," *New York
                       Times*, September 5, 2004.

Mortimer B.   "The Elusive Mideast Peace," *U.S.
Zuckerman   News & World Report*, January 28,
                       2008.

Index